The Magic of Purbeck

The Magic of Purbeck

David Leadbetter

Roving Press

© 2015 David Leadbetter

Published by Roving Press Ltd
4 Southover Cottages, Frampton, Dorset, DT2 9NQ, UK
Tel: 01300 321531
www.rovingpress.co.uk

First published 2015 by Roving Press Ltd

ISBN: 978-1-906651-251

British Library Cataloguing in Publication Data
A catalogue record for this book is available from the British Library

Cover design by Tim Mc...

Maps created by ... Johns Ltd. Based upon Ordnance Survey digital map data
© Crown Copyright 2015 Licence Number 433680. All rights reserved.

Set in 11.5/13 p...
Printed and bound by Henry Ling Ltd, The Dorset Press, Dorchester, DT1 1HD

Contents

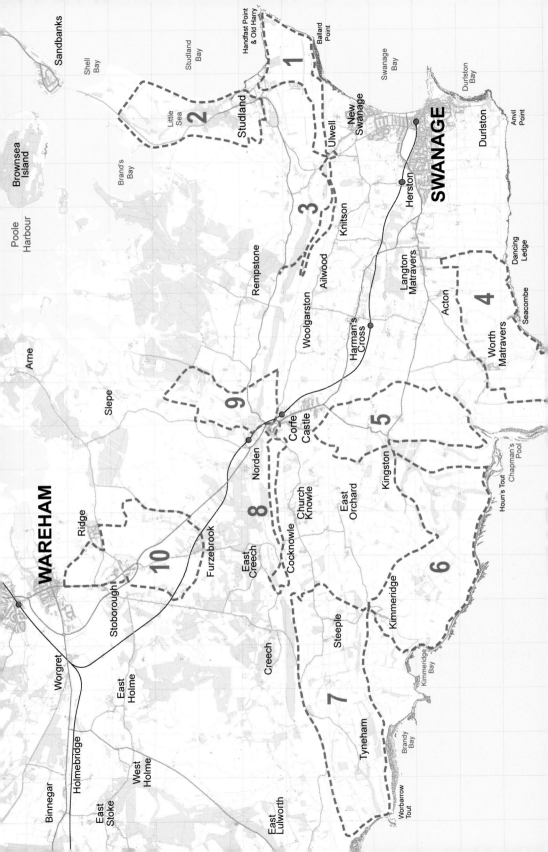

Preface

Walking is one of the healthiest activities that can be engaged in and is popular for a number of reasons. As well as the obvious physical benefits, there is a spiritual dimension that can be obtained from uplifting views of beautiful places, reducing stress and tension that accrue from our busy lives. A walk can also be an opportunity to learn something new, whether details of local history or putting a name to some of the plants and animals encountered. While walking can be a solitary pursuit, it is good to share interests with others and meet those who are like-minded; it is therefore an excellent way of bringing people together.

The Isle of Purbeck has stunning, varied scenery within a small geographical area, as well as a wide range of fauna and flora and rich local history. The aim of this book is to introduce some of the features that make the area such a special place, hopefully inspiring the walker to experience some of the 'magic' of Purbeck. The walks vary in length and cover a variety of terrain. Maps are provided for each walk, though an Ordnance Survey map is also recommended. Many of the walks can be adapted to suit the individual, who may wish to do a section of the route or even go further. All can be accessed by local buses, though Walk 7 is best done from the car park north-east of Kimmeridge.

Of interest to local people as well as visitors, while some walks may be familiar, the unique combination of features described is likely to introduce the reader/ walker to new aspects and raise awareness of how special Purbeck is. As well as geological features there are details of where to find some of Purbeck's notable birds, plants and butterflies – the author has focused on these groups as they tend to be the most obvious, though other taxa are also described, and there are identification guides listed in the References.

Descriptions of historical and archaeological features are given, with special reference to barrows, unusual burials, standing stones, strip lynchets and churches. Mention is made of archaeological excavations and findings and also the derivation of place names. A special feature of the book is the introductory chapters on local geology, natural history and local history; with regard to the latter, the author has concentrated on the prehistoric era and Roman Conquest as these are less well known than later periods.

Whatever your interests, my message is: enjoy walking in Purbeck and discover the magic for yourself.

Special thanks are due to my publishers Julie and Tim Musk for all their hard work on the text, photographs and maps to produce a first-class effort; also Christine Bowman-Hill for reading the text and making helpful suggestions.

David Leadbetter

Geology and Natural History

Geology

The first reference to Purbeck occurs in an Old English charter of 948 describing land granted to Corfe Castle, where the area is referred to as 'Purbicinga'. 'Pur' probably means 'bittern' or 'snipe' and 'bica' a bill or beak, the name suggesting that the chalk ridge running west to east could resemble a Bittern's beak.

The Isle of Purbeck is not strictly speaking an island but is, more or less, surrounded by water of some kind. To the south and east lie open sea, while on the north-eastern side, Poole Harbour, the second largest natural harbour in the world, forms a backdrop. The River Frome acts as the northern boundary, and in the west a small stream known as Luckford Lake, with its source north of Worbarrow Bay, flows northwards to the Frome to complete the insular impression.

The view from Kingswood Down along the Purbeck Way.

This relatively small area has a remarkably varied geology, which in turn has resulted in a special landscape and habitats for different species. It is therefore not surprising that Purbeck is a designated Area of Outstanding Natural Beauty, nor that there are National Nature Reserves at Studland and Godlingston Heaths, Hartland Moor, Stoborough Heath, Durlston Country Park and Arne reedbeds. In 2001 the Dorset and East Devon coast was declared a World Heritage Site as it is the best example in the world of a continuous geological record for 185 million years – from the Triassic to Cretaceous periods.

Godlingston Heath National Nature Reserve.

There are six main rock formations in Purbeck, starting with the oldest in the south, running north to the most recent deposits. The earliest is **Kimmeridge Clay**, laid down on a tropical sea bed about 155 million years ago (mya), exposed well at Kimmeridge Bay and Chapman's Pool; the rock is famous for fossils, the ancient shale industry and modern oil extraction (Walk 6). On higher ground in south Purbeck, Kimmeridge Clay is overlain by **Portland and Purbeck Limestones**. Portland Limestone, formed about 145 mya, is a high-quality building stone and was quarried locally at Dancing Ledge, Seacombe and Winspit (Walk 4).

The Purbeck Beds (about 145–135 mya) consist of limestones and clays and are a freshwater deposit laid down in mud in lagoons and swamps, forming much of the plateau running west from Durlston Bay to Worbarrow Tout. They include Purbeck Marble, used since Roman times, building stone used for local cottages and drystone

Winspit geology.

walls, and fossil finds such as rare mammals at Durlston, crocodiles, turtles, dinosaur footprints in quarries and tree trunks at Lulworth.

The central valley of Purbeck lies immediately north of the limestone plateau and is composed of **Wealden Clay**, consisting of soft clays and sands that are easily eroded, as can be seen from cliffs at Swanage and Worbarrow Bays. Between the Wealden and chalk ridge to the north lies a narrow band of Greensand and Gault Clay, best seen at Punfield Cove at the north-west end of Swanage Bay.

The fifth main rock formation is the **Chalk**, running in a narrow ridge from Old Harry to Lulworth and laid down about 100–65 mya, formed from tiny shells of micro-organisms that accumulated on the seabed.

Handfast Point and Old Harry.

A narrow strip of Reading Beds and London Clay is found north of the chalk ridge before the last major deposit, the **Bagshot Beds** (about 45 mya) is reached; these consist of clays and sands and form the large track of heathland stretching west and north from Studland. The fine clay was used to make pottery in prehistoric and Roman times as well as more recently. The heathland also contains an irony sandstone and it is this that forms the imposing Agglestone Rock.

The Agglestone stands out prominently on Godlingston Heath.

During much of the time when the rock formations of Purbeck were being deposited, the area was submerged, but around 35 mya the land gradually thrust upwards due to movements in the Earth's crust (the same movement that formed the Alps when Africa collided with Europe). Parts of Ballard Down experienced violent tilting in the rocks; some of the chalk beds became vertical and a major fault, known as Ballard Down Fault (viewable by boat), occurred. Gaps in the Purbeck Hills at Ulwell and Corfe Castle are a result of the fracturing in the chalk.

Natural History

The Jurassic coast from Durlston Head west to Worbarrow Bay consists of steep, rugged cliffs, with the only accessible beaches being Durlston (very rocky), Chapman's Pool (sometimes closed due to landslides), Kimmeridge and Worbarrow (subject to Army Range opening times). The sheer limestone cliffs between Durlston and St Aldhelm's Head make ideal homes for seabirds, with hundreds of Guillemots (the highest concentration at Durlston), small numbers of Razorbills and a handful of Puffins at Dancing Ledge. Shags, Fulmars, Herring Gulls and Great Black-backed Gulls also breed along the coast, with nesting Cormorants confined to Gad Cliff and Kittiwakes east of Dancing Ledge at Blackers Hole. Other birds to take advantage of nesting

Along the Purbeck coast: a view of Chapman's Pool and Emmetts Hill from Houns-tout.

opportunities include Peregrine and Raven. Bird migration is often evident along this stretch of coast, with Durlston, Winspit Valley and St Aldhelm's Head being hot spots. Butterfly migration may also be visible – Clouded Yellows, Red Admirals, Painted Ladies and Large and Small Whites make landfall along the coast and may be joined by day-flying Humming Bird Hawk-moths.

Characteristic plants of these cliffs include Thrift, Wild Cabbage, Golden Samphire, Rock Samphire and Sea Aster. The beach at Kimmeridge with its rocky pools offers an ideal introduction to marine life (Walk 6) and the Fine Foundation Marine Centre has interesting displays. While walking along the coast, it is worth keeping an eye on the sea itself as Gannets pass by regularly, particularly in

Golden Samphire at Hedbury.

windy conditions, and you may even be rewarded by seeing a pod of Bottle-nosed Dolphins.

Away from the cliffs, the limestone plateau between Durlston Bay and Tyneham is largely devoid of trees, apart from several attractive woods north of Langton and certain areas of planted woodland such as near Kingston. Skylarks are still a common sight and sound in Purbeck. Birds of prey such as Buzzard, Kestrel and Peregrine are also regular. Hares may occasionally be seen in grassland in less-frequented areas, while the lucky observer may spot a Stoat or Weasel; the most likely mammal sightings, apart from the ubiquitous Rabbit, will be Roe Deer and Fox, while Badger setts are fairly evident.

The short limestone turf attracts a selection of butterflies, most notably Adonis Blue, Dingy Skipper, Lulworth Skipper and Wall; there is a small colony of Grizzled Skipper at Durlston and Small Blue may be seen there as well as at Townsend Reserve. The south side of the Wilderness north of Langton can produce White-letter and Purple Hairstreaks for the patient observer with binoculars. Many plants are characteristic of dry limestone grassland such as Horseshoe Vetch, Chalk Milkwort, Wild Clary, Fiddle Dock and Salad Burnet, but the one that botanists from miles around come to see is Early Spider Orchid, with its best colonies in Purbeck, particularly around Dancing Ledge (Walk 4), where thousands may flower in a good year.

The central valley of Purbeck, consisting of Wealden Clay, is fertile farming land and a number of farms were established close to the spring line south of the chalk ridge. One accessible area of particular interest to the wildlife enthusiast is Corfe Common (Walk 5), which may have been grazed for centuries. The Common is especially noted for its wild flowers, some of which are scarce; in wetter areas, Southern Marsh Orchid, Heath Spotted Orchid, Lousewort and Lady's Smock are found, while drier parts produce Betony, Chamomile and Devil's-bit Scabious, with an abundance of Bluebells on higher parts of West Common.

Corfe Common.

The chalk ridge stretching from Old Harry to Lulworth forms the spine of Purbeck and is a much narrower band than the limestone further south. Southern slopes are rich in butterflies and Ballard Down (Walk 1) boasts over 30 different species, with major populations of Adonis Blue and Dingy Skipper, smaller numbers of Wall, Brown Argus and Dark Green Fritillary, as well as migrants such as Clouded Yellow. This is also a good area to see grasshoppers and crickets, with a number of species present including the Great Green Bush-cricket. Stonechats, Dartford Warblers and Common Whitethroats breed on Ballard, with birds of prey and Ravens frequently overhead. The song of the Skylark is a common sound on these hills. In spring and autumn, birds migrating through may be encountered along the ridge.

The chalk flora is equally rich and many species found on limestone can also be seen here, though Early Spider Orchid is not normally encountered and Chalk Milkwort is less frequent. Rare Nottingham Catchfly (Walk 1) only occurs on the chalk. Mention must also be made of three woods on the north side of the ridge: Studland Wood (Walk 1), King's Wood (Walk 3) and Stonehill Down (Walk 8); these are especially beautiful in spring, with a range of plant species.

The expanse of heathland to the north of the chalk was created in the Neolithic and Bronze Ages through tree clearance by man and maintained by subsequent grazing and fuel burning. Although the soils are acidic and contain fewer species, some of Britain's rarest animals and plants are found on lowland heaths, itself an increasingly rare habitat.

The heath is home to three particular species of birds, all of which seem to be on the increase: the resident Dartford Warbler, though it has spread to other habitats, has its stronghold among gorse-clad heaths; and the Nightjar and Hobby are both summer visitors, the former only seen at dusk or night-time, while the latter hunts dragonflies in the day, catching them in the air. More types of dragonflies and damselflies occur near boggy pools and stretches of water on heathland than on any other habitat, and in Purbeck a range of species may be encountered including Hairy Dragonfly, Downy Emerald, Ruddy Darter, Small Red Damselfly and Southern Damselfly. All six native species of reptile are found here, including populations of rare Smooth Snake and Sand Lizard.

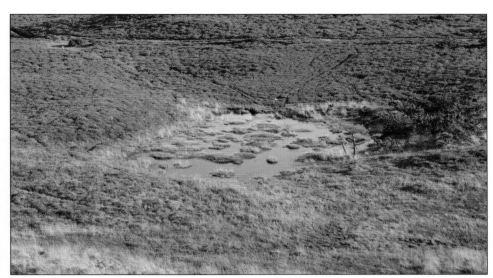

Boggy pool on Godlingston Heath.

Little Sea.

Dry heathland has few species of plants – mostly gorses and heathers – but wet areas have a number of rare species, including Marsh Gentian, Dorset Heath, Bog Orchid and three species of sundew, with Yellow Centaury, Allseed and Chaffweed on a few damp tracks and Bog Asphodel in wetter areas. Otters have returned to the Studland area, but one of the most frequently seen mammals is Japanese Sika Deer, originally introduced to Brownsea Island in 1896.

One other habitat needs to be mentioned – the beaches and shores around Studland (Walk 2). Birdwatching can be good in winter, particularly along shores and bays west of Ferry Road which are much less disturbed than Shell Bay and Studland Beach. Brand's Bay can be productive for many species of waders (including Avocet), Brent Geese and ducks. Between Brand's Bay and Bramble Bush Bay Little Egrets and Grey Herons are likely to be encountered, and fast-running Sanderlings are sometimes a feature of the shore around the latter bay. Offshore there is often a good selection of grebes, Red-breasted Merganser, Goldeneye, Great Northern Diver and the occasional rarity; similar species (not usually Goldeneye) can be seen from Shell Bay and Studland Beach, and Cormorants and Shags are frequent there.

Beautiful Studland Beach, 4 miles of white sand, and heath, a haven for wildlife.

Brand's Bay.

Appropriately named Shell Bay is good for sea shells, as is Studland Beach; up to 50 species may be found. Roots of Marram and Lyme-grass help stabilise dunes at Studland, and scarce plants such as Sea Bindweed and Prickly Saltwort occur at the edge of dunes near the beach.

Priest's Way stone

Purbeck Through History

Throughout this book reference is made to 'prehistoric' as well as later historical sites, so an overview of these periods as they relate to Purbeck now follows:

Palaeolithic: *c* 900,000–9600 BCE
Mesolithic: *c* 9600–4400 BCE
Neolithic: *c* 4400–2200 BCE
Bronze Age: *c* 2200–700 BCE
Iron Age: *c* 700 BCE to 43 CE

The Palaeolithic covers a vast period when the climate fluctuated between intensely cold glacial and warmer interglacial periods. During glacial maxima, sea-levels were up to 120 m lower and much of what is now the English Channel and North Sea were then land, while in the warmer interglacials sea-levels were sometimes higher than today. When climatic conditions were suitable, hunter-gatherers roamed in search of food, probably following seasonal herds such as Mammoths and Reindeer, so permanent camps were unlikely. During the coldest periods Britain may have been uninhabited for thousands of years. The appearance of 'Purbeck' would have been very different from today: the chalk ridge did not end at Ballard Head but was joined eastwards to the Isle of Wight, with the sea making incursions in the ridge between 90,000 and 75,000 years ago when sea-levels were 7.5 m higher than today. A wide river valley lay north of Purbeck stretching from the modern Frome valley to the Solent, with the ancient river, sometimes referred to as the Solent River, flowing eastwards.

Hunter-gatherers from these times no doubt visited Purbeck but have left few traces. Flint hand axes preserved in gravels laid down by rivers such as the Frome are a good source of evidence of early man's presence. One such Palaeolithic axe found on the beach of Furzey Island (note that Furzey and Green Islands were often joined to the Ower peninsula in prehistoric times) came from a gravel deposit, but it is not clear whether it was dropped there or transported by the sea. At the end of the Palaeolithic a seasonal camp was established at Hengistbury Head (around 12,000–11,000 BCE) and it is possible that some of these people visited Purbeck.

Inhabitants of Mesolithic Dorset were mainly nomadic, with permanent camps identified at Portland and Hengistbury, and the shore line was many miles to the south of the present ones at Hengistbury and Poole Harbour. A detailed archaeological survey of sites in northern Purbeck between Poole Harbour and the chalk ridge from 1987 to 1990 in conjunction with development of Wytch

Farm oilfield concluded that there was only intermittent occupation during the Mesolithic in Purbeck, with a few finds from a number of locations. The most important seem to have been south of this area at Blashenwell (Walk 5) and Ulwell (Walk 1), where a few flint tools and marine molluscs were found, suggesting the possibility of seasonal camps. A temporary camp may also have been established on the eastern bank of Corfe River north of Corfe Castle, as flint finds suggest. Nearby, at Bestwall, east of Wareham, there is also evidence of a temporary camp.

The Neolithic period was a time of great innovation, though probably gradual. Monuments such as causewayed enclosures, long barrows, bank barrows, henges and cursuses were constructed. These suggest a veneration for ancestors and some of the alignments of the monuments indicate the importance attached to the Moon and Sun. The long barrow on Ailwood Down (Walk 3) is likely to date to the Early Neolithic, while the oval barrow on Stonehill Down (Walk 8) may be later; it was usual for early long barrows to contain the remains of a number of dead in the form of disarticulated bones, but later ones often had articulated skeletons and were mainly male. The first round barrows may date to the later Neolithic but will be covered under the Bronze Age section.

The Neolithic period in Britain is associated with the arrival of farming and a more sedentary way of life. From about 3900 BCE there were extensive forest clearances and the Wytch Farm Project found that in the northern half of Purbeck there was selective felling of mainly Lime and Scots Pine in the Early Neolithic, followed by more clearance of Lime, Oak and Hazel, with some Beech and Ash, later on. The first settlers in Purbeck may well have farmed the fertile Wealden valley and possibly the chalk ridge, so some forest clearance there was

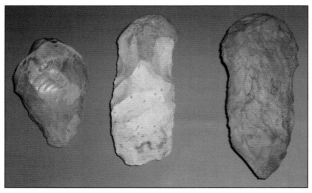

Neolithic hand axes found in Purbeck. (Courtesy of Langton Matravers and Purbeck Stone Museum.)

also likely. Early farmers in Britain used axes made of flint or hard igneous rock to help with clearance, though some axes seem to have had a ceremonial significance. Pottery was used for the first time and sherds from Worth Matravers have been dated to 3600 BCE; the ditch they were in may have been part of a Neolithic causeway.

In the Later Neolithic the focus of activity appears to have been on New Mills Heath, shown by finds of worked flints, but any settlement may have been near the river and its tributaries. Evidence has been found of Neolithic activity at Bestwall near the River Frome (see Bestwall Quarry Excavation Project).

There is no clear division between the Late Neolithic and Early Bronze Age, with some metal working occurring at the end of the Neolithic and stone axes sometimes copied from bronze prototypes from the Continent. The 'Beaker' people first appear in the Late Neolithic, named after their distinctive and often highly decorated drinking vessels frequently placed in graves. The Early Beaker phase (2800–2000 BCE) saw the building of huge henge enclosures at Avebury, Stonehenge and Durrington Walls. Rempstone Stone Circle (Walk 3) may date to this period. Early Beaker burials were often of individuals placed in a crouched position under a round barrow, sometimes accompanied by grave goods. The Ulwell barrow (Walk 1) and primary inhumation probably date to this period, as well as the oak log burial found in King's Barrow at Stoborough (Walk 10). Later in the Bronze Age, cremation became more common and barrows often appear in clusters to form cemeteries (Walk 3, Ailwood Down).

Barrows on Ailwood Down.

There are different types of round barrow, with the commonest being bowl shaped surrounded by a ditch. Purbeck also has examples of bell barrows (Walk 2) and one pond barrow (Walk 1). While many Purbeck barrows are located on downland, quite a number are found on the heaths. It should be noted that some contain later inhumations and cremations as well as the original 'primary' burial. By 1400 BCE cremation was the dominant rite, no doubt reflecting a change in belief, and barrow construction declined, with cremated remains being placed in urns, some of which were inserted in barrows.

In the Early–Middle Bronze Age there was extensive clearance of woodland on the heaths, as shown by acidification of the soil, and by the end of the period heathland flora was well established. From the Middle Bronze Age the landscape became more planned, with large field systems and long linear boundaries. Bronze Age field systems have been discovered at the East of Corfe River site and New Mills Heath, showing intensive agricultural use, and it is thought there was a move into this area around 1500 BCE following overexploitation of the chalk downland. However, the field system was soon abandoned due to deterioration of the soil.

There is evidence from the Late Bronze Age of several occupation sites in south Purbeck. The settlement at Eldon's Seat (Walk 5) consisted of several round houses, with a developing field system and manufacture of Kimmeridge shale armlets; occupation lasted well into the Iron Age. Another at Rope Lake Hole dates from a similar period, with even more emphasis on industrial activities. There were also workshops at Kimmeridge itself. A Late Bronze Age round house was found at Worth, and dating from the Late Bronze/Early Iron Age a large cobbled area used as a meeting place (Walk 4). Clay was clearly being exploited throughout the Bronze Age, as a huge range of pots were produced at Bestwall, where settlements spanned seven to eight centuries. Finally, the largest ever Bronze Age axe-head hoard in Britain was found near Langton Matravers in 2007 (Walk 4), and dated to about 800 BCE, with a probable settlement nearby.

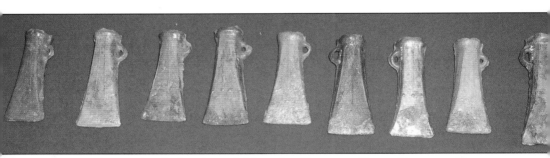

Bronze Age axe heads found in a field south of Langton village. (Courtesy of Langton Matravers and Purbeck Stone Museum.)

The Iron Age saw a transition from bronze to iron and the construction of hill forts. Purbeck's only hill fort is Flower's Barrow (Walk 8), part of which has fallen into the sea.

Away from the hill forts, the typical rural settlement consisted of a small farmstead supporting a family, or sometimes an extended one; the farm would be surrounded by an earthwork and usually near an ancient field system. The term 'Celtic fields' is used for all fields laid out before the Saxon conquest, consisting of small rectilinear paddocks joined together resembling a chequerboard.

The Eldon Seat settlement continued well into the Iron Age, with the size of the house increasing; sheep became more important than cattle (small Celtic short-horns) by the 6th century, reflecting a trend throughout Wessex. The Kimmeridge shale industry became more developed with the introduction of lathe-turning in the 1st century, and salt production was taking place at Kimmeridge, Hobarrow Bay and Rope Lake Hole in the Early Iron Age.

Purbeck has the greatest concentration of Iron Age and Romano-British sites in Dorset and there have been pottery finds from a number of locations;

at Gallows Gore 14 storage pits were also found. Towards the end of the Middle Iron Age, Furzey Island (not then an island), Shipstal Point and Fitzworth all had settlements probably linked to salt production; an Iron Age log boat found in Poole Harbour has been dated to 295 BCE and can be seen in Poole Museum.

Poole Harbour was becoming an important centre for trade by the 1st century, judging by the finds of imported goods, though the main port at this time was Hengistbury. There was a considerable increase in activity and density of occupation at the East of Corfe River site and Ower Peninsula in the Late Iron Age; at the former there was an extensive settlement, with evidence of agriculture, salt working and possibly pottery production, while there was intensive shale working at Ower, which may have been a production centre. On the west bank of Corfe River a possible pottery production site with a firing structure was found; high-quality ball clay occurs nearby. In addition to these sites, considerable amounts of salt, pottery and shale items were produced at Cleaval Point, Green Island, Fitzworth, Middlebere and Shipstal Point. An apparent causeway (dated to *c* 250–200 BCE) between Cleaval Point and Green Island is now believed to have been a breakwater, acting as shelter for boats and enabling them to unload cargoes.

The Durotriges occupied most of what is now modern Dorset and south Somerset at the time of the Roman Conquest. As a tribe they are loosely connected by three elements: distinctive pottery known as black burnished ware, with simple decoration, centred around Poole Harbour (an important site has been found at Worgret, west of Wareham); their own coinage from about 50 BCE; and crouched burials on the right side, usually with the head orientated to the east, and grave goods. Pig bones often accompanied female burials, cattle with male, and sheep with both.

In 2004, 142 base-metal Durotrigan staters (based on ancient coins used in Greece) were discovered at Norden and dated from 1 to 50 CE; many have small test marks on their surface, suggesting they were deposited as an offering. In 2006 a Late Iron Age stone temple 4 m^2 was also located at Norden and its construction trench contained Durotrigan pottery, coins, two spearheads and other ironwork, indicating some kind of dedication.

In 43 CE the Romans invaded Britain. In Purbeck it would seem local communities may have been willing to work with them from the beginning. Norden became a major

Durotrigan coins and patera from Norden. (Courtesy of Dorset County Museum.)

manufacturing centre between the 1st and 4th centuries, specialising in high-quality goods such as chalk tesserae, elaborate shale items and Purbeck Marble mortaria (small bowls used for mixing or grinding food). A magnetometer survey has shown there was a major Romano-British road connecting the site. It is possible the industrial complex at Norden may have developed from the temple mentioned above.

Black burnished ware was being produced in huge quantities by the early 2nd century, with the Worgret site, which appears to have developed from a Durotrigan settlement, perhaps manufacturing this pottery to the exclusion of all else; the site was close to the River Frome with access to Dorchester, not far from Poole Harbour, and it may have been linked to Norden by the Roman road. The pottery consisted of plain kitchen ware made by hand and finished by burnishing the surface with a bone polisher. In Dorset it was used far more than any other kitchen ware and was favoured by the Roman army, with large amounts being exported to the north, including Hadrian's Wall where half the pottery found is Durotrigan. By the Late Roman period large-scale iron smelting was taking place by the Frome not far from Worgret.

Durotrigan black burnished ware. (Courtesy of Dorset County Museum.)

At the same time as the rise in importance of sites at Norden and Worgret, industrial settlements at Ower Peninsula and East of Corfe River reduced in size by the late 1st century and reverted to agriculture. Three Roman villas have been found within a few miles of Norden: East Creech (Walk 8), Bucknowle (Walk 5) and Brenscombe (Walk 9); all may have developed from Late Iron Age sites and were probably based on agriculture, though shale furniture was produced at Bucknowle and a ritual site from the Middle Iron Age was also identified here. Many rural settlements, in fact, show continuity between the Late Iron Age and Roman periods, while some new ones would have been established. The Romano-British settlement at Woodhouse, Studland (Walk 1), showed evidence of occupation for much of the Roman period.

Soon after the Roman invasion, Purbeck Marble began to be quarried at Wilkswood for inscriptions, wall inlays and mouldings; large amounts were used in the palace of Fishbourne, Hampshire, and in a number of Roman towns. Kimmeridge shale bracelets were being produced in great numbers on lathes at rural sites such as Rope Lake Hole. The Iron Age and Romano-British settlement at Quarry Field, Worth, also showed evidence of shale armlet working – both hand worked and lathe produced; two crouched Durotrigan burials were excavated, the graves being aligned in a mirror image (Walk 4). In 2011, 17 or 18 infant burials were found near a Roman barn close by. Some Durotrigan burial rites and the use of coinage continued well into the Roman period. In Purbeck there are also several unusual female burials, one of which dates to the late 3rd century (Walk 6) where the skull and jaw were removed and placed in a different position.

Within a few decades of the end of Roman rule and withdrawal from Britain in 410, the market economy had collapsed. The Saxon advance into Dorset did not occur until the mid-6th century. Industrial activity appears to have largely ceased in Purbeck in the Saxon period, though rural settlements may have continued much as before and farming would have become more important.

There is little archaeological evidence for the 5th–7th centuries, apart from two cemeteries: the one at Worth (Walk 4) consisted of 26 burials in an approximate east–west alignment, with the only grave good being a buckle dated to the mid-6th century, while the other at Ulwell (Walk 1) containing at least 57 burials, also in a mainly east–west orientation, was dated to the 7th century and several Roman finds may suggest continuity of Romano-British traditions. In both cases the relative lack of grave goods and orientation of inhumations suggest they may have been early Christian; it is known Christianity had become established in Wessex in the 4th century.

In Lady St Mary's Church, Wareham, stone inscriptions in Latin dating from the 7th–9th centuries also indicate survival of a Christian British enclave; Saxons began to arrive after the year 650, and around 700 St Aldhelm, the first bishop of the West Saxons, founded a nunnery and church at Wareham. There was also a church built in Purbeck at this time, probably at Corfe. Wareham became a town of importance, with West Saxon King Beorhtric buried in the church in 802. The town's first defensive walls were built in the 9th century and it is recorded that a Danish force occupied Wareham in 876, with 120 ships wrecked off Swanage in a storm the following year. By 900 Wareham was the fourth largest town in Wessex and in the reign of King Athelstan (924–39) it was granted permission to mint coins.

Corfe Castle also saw dramatic historical events, with the murder of King Edward in 978 on his stepmother's orders so her own son Ethelred could become king; the royal residence at Corfe was probably where the castle now stands.

In the later Saxon and medieval periods Purbeck's economic development was closely connected to its status as a Royal Chase; the Church also had an important role, with large areas of the southern shores of Poole Harbour being owned by Milton, Shaftesbury and Cerne Abbeys. In the 10th century Corfe was a royal estate, covering east Purbeck, which was being subdivided, and some place names in east Purbeck may derive from the person who held the land; many place names in west Purbeck are topographical. England was now

Corfe Castle.

divided into 'shires', which were subdivided into 'hundreds' where courts met. Purbeck had two hundreds: Rowbarrow and Hasler; the former met at a barrow in Woolgarston, the latter at a barrow in a Hazel wood in Steeple.

The Norman Conquest of 1066 marked another turning point in British history, with the destruction of the Anglo-Saxon nobility, restructuring of society along feudal lines and building of great castles and churches. In the *Domesday Book* of 1086 Purbeck was placed in the second highest national valuation band of 40–80 shillings per square mile, but by 1334 it had become a poor area, being placed in the second lowest national band for assessed wealth; intensive farming was taking place across the limestone plateau, as shown by strip lynchets near Worth and other places, but the land was not best quality for agriculture. Many Purbeck villages and farms are named in *Domesday* and some of these names go back to Saxon times.

Purbeck Marble, which had not been used since Roman times, began to be quarried again from the 1140s and used extensively for interior work in cathedrals and churches, including pillars, effigies, coffin lids and fonts. The height of the industry was from the mid-13th to mid-14th centuries and West Street, Corfe, became the focus of marble workshops, with worked material being transported to Ower Quay. The early Norman period saw the building of three churches in Purbeck – at Studland (Walk 1), Worth (Walk 4) and Steeple – with Studland being the finest remaining example.

The dominant building in the area would undoubtedly have been Corfe Castle, with the keep being early 12th century. The southern shores of Poole

Purbeck Marble inside St James's Church, Kingston.

Harbour were used for salt extraction around the mid-13th and 14th centuries and processing of fish and shellfish took place at times; some of this probably went to the abbeys that owned the land. King John (1199–1216), a frequent visitor to Purbeck, is said to have had three hunting lodges built: at Creech Barrow Hill (Walk 8), Swanage (perhaps Windmill Hill) and Slepe.

As much has been written about the more recent history of Purbeck, the main trends only are noted here. Purbeck Marble was in decline by the 16th century, but the quarrying of Purbeck and Portland Limestone was soon to gather momentum and by the 19th century became a major industry, with stone shipped from Swanage to supply building work in London by John Mowlem's firm. There were underground and cliff-top quarries as well as open cast (Walks 4 and 5). Pottery production was largely discontinued after the Romano-British period, but from the 18th century onwards ball-clay was exploited at a number of sites north of the chalk ridge. The Pike Brothers set up a base at Furzebrook with their outlet at Ridge, while rival Benjamin Fayle bought Norden clay pits (Walk 10) and later opened a clay works at Newton. In the 20th century oil extraction from beneath the shale began at Kimmeridge (Walk 6) and later the largest inland deposit of oil in Britain was discovered at Wytch Farm. Undoubtedly, the most important modern source of income today to local people is tourism.

In 1959 Kimmeridge Oil Well (part of Wytch Farm oil field) started production on the cliff-top above Kimmeridge Bay. The nodding donkey still pumps oil at a rate of about 100 barrels a day.

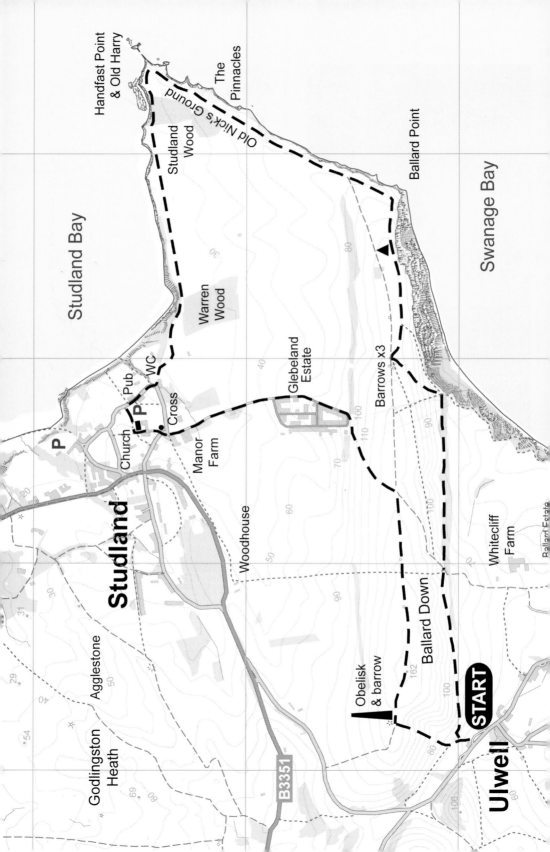

Walk 1:
Ulwell Gap, Ballard Down, Old Harry and Studland

An area rich in fauna and flora, geology and ancient history, with spectacular views from Ballard Down

Distance: approx. 6 miles

Best time to do: late April to late September

Refreshments: Village Inn, Ulwell, and several locations in Studland

Parking: in lay-bys at Ulwell on Studland–Swanage road (SZ 022809)

Suggested route: from Ulwell follow Purbeck Way to Old Harry and Studland, returning via Glebeland Estate along Ballard Down hilltop to Obelisk

The area at the start of the walk, where the busy Swanage–Studland road runs through Ulwell gap, was inhabited in ancient times. In 1931 when the road was being widened **Mesolithic flint tools** were found and a small pit containing periwinkles, cockles and limpets. Mesolithic finds are rare in Purbeck and it is thought that prehistoric people from this period were mainly nomadic, though the finds here may indicate a seasonal camp.

Ulwell used to have a mill and the name may derive from 'Ule wella', a well, spring or stream frequented by owls, or 'holy well'. In the Iron Age and Romano-British periods springs were regarded as sacred and votive offerings were made to gods and goddesses here.

At Shepherd's Farm near the lay-by a **7th-century inhumation cemetery** was discovered in 1982: 57 burials, some in earth graves, others in cists (box-shaped burial chambers made of stone slabs), consisted of men, women and children. The burials occurred over several generations and it is possible from the lack of grave goods and general east–west alignment they were Christian rather than Pagan. From the number of graves it would appear there was a settlement nearby, though no trace has been found; there would have been a plentiful water supply from the stream here.

Ballard Down is the name given to the eastern end of the chalk hills that extend from Lulworth and Flower's Barrow above Worbarrow Bay in the west of Purbeck. There are two natural gaps in this range: one at Corfe Castle, the other here at Ulwell.

From the lay-by opposite the caravan park take the footpath right along the base of Ballard Down, following the Purbeck Way. The lower slopes have a profusion of flowers in spring and summer and it is one of the best sites in

Ballard Down viewed from Swanage.

Purbeck for butterflies, with up to 25 species recorded in August. Being south-facing, species emerge earlier than at other sites. Purbeck is one of the remaining strongholds in Britain for the **Adonis Blue**, which may emerge in hundreds in favourable years (there are two broods: May/June and Aug/ Sept). It requires short turf and warm south-facing slopes, and its food plant is the **Horseshoe Vetch**. The more purple-blue **Common Blue** favours longer grass at the bottom of the downs, while the **Holly Blue** typically flies higher around the hedgerows.

Adonis Blue.

The Adonis Blue has a special relationship with ants, which offer protection to the caterpillar, even burying it in loose soil for the night and mounting guard; in return the caterpillar exudes sweet secretions and emits a kind of song, which appears to excite the ants. The chrysalis may sometimes be found in the ants' nest and also produces chemical substances and noises. This relationship has been observed in other species of blues and is an excellent example of symbiosis.

The **Green Hairstreak** is another butterfly seen here, and its chrysalis is also attractive to ants because of the noise it makes. It is usually on the wing late April–June and frequently rests on shrubs near the track, taking off in spiralling flight when disturbed, displaying its green underwings; it is the only British species to have this colour and it has the widest range of food plants of any of our butterflies. **Dingy Skipper**, **Brown Argus** and **Wall** may also be seen on this walk as well as more common species.

Horseshoe Vetch and **Bird's-foot Trefoil** both take their name from their seedpod shape. **Common Gromwell, Bladder Campion** and **Cowslip** may be found near the start of the track and **Crosswort** is common near the bottom path east of Ulwell, where its tiny yellow flowers in the shape of a cross can be seen in spring. Later in summer, characteristic plants of chalk such as **Vervain, Marjoram, Yellow-wort, Rockrose, Ploughman's Spikenard, Pyramidal Orchid** and **Common Centaury** may be seen on the lower slopes, with **Marjoram** particularly attractive to butterflies.

Gorse is abundant here, and if lucky you might see **Dartford Warbler** perched on a bush, or more likely flitting about. **Common Whitethroats**, closely related to Dartford Warblers, are present during spring and summer and their scratchy jangle, sometimes delivered in the air, is diagnostic. You may also hear the monotonous rattle of **Lesser Whitethroats** calling in spring as they pass through on migration. It is worth keeping an eye on the sky as **Buzzard, Kestrel, Raven, Peregrine** and **Sparrowhawk** are frequent.

Just before the path reaches Whitecliff there is a patch of nettles to the right below the track where **Badgers** have made a sett for many years; entrances are also sometimes present in the field beyond.

The Purbeck Way crosses a steep path with loose flints and continues east with a gradual ascent; it is uneven in places and slippery after rain. **Whitecliff Farm** below to the south-west is referred to in *Domesday* as 'Witeclive', taking its name from the nearby white cliffs. The present farmhouse is partly 16th century.

The path above Whitecliff Farm.

After approximately 400 m the track crosses scrub and emerges onto short turf. Continue on the Purbeck Way. Endemic **Early Gentian** grows here, best looked for in late May. It can be erratic in appearance; the small purple flowers open in sun and the plant is only a few centimetres high.

Early Gentian.

As you walk along the path and climb higher, the panorama of Swanage stretches out below. The fields and cliffs at Swanage are composed of **Wealden Clay** and there have been serious cliff falls. Swanage Bay was formed as a result of erosion of the soft clay, which lies between the Chalk to the north, on which you are standing, and Purbeck and Portland Limestone beds to the south.

Swanage Bay from Ballard Down.

An interesting plant to look for further along the path is **Early Purple Orchid**, blooming mid-April– May. Later in summer **Autumn Lady's-tresses Orchid** and **Carline Thistle** may be seen.

Carline Thistle.

Early Purple Orchid.

Carry on along the upper path and Purbeck Way, climbing to the top of the hill before continuing eastwards through a gate. Just before the gate are two Bronze Age **bowl barrows** and a few metres north a shallow depression, a **pond barrow**. All three barrows were excavated by John Austen in 1857. One contained the remains of two skeletons: the primary burial at about 2.5 m deep was of a tall person about 1.8 m high, placed in a crouched position and covered with lumps of chalk, with a piece of deer antler near the head. The secondary burial was 0.6 m deep and the skeleton, laid out straight, was only 1.2 m long, suggesting a young person. The other bowl barrow contained skeletons of a tall person in a crouched position and an infant. Austen did not discover much in the pond barrow, but more recent excavations have revealed a few burnt remains.

Bowl barrows at the top of Ballard Down.

Further on is a trig point and some depressions and mounds (possibly caused by WWII activity). **Skylarks** are common here and in spring their musical notes are likely to accompany you as you proceed towards the cliffs. They are ground-nesting birds and suffer disturbance from dogs that are not under control.

Keep on down the grassy slope with the Needles on the Isle of Wight straight ahead across the sea. On a clear day the coastline north-east offers excellent views. As you approach Ballard Point down the sloping path, look out for the rare **Nottingham Catchfly** (late May–July); this sticky member of the Campion family has small white flowers and grows in grassland near and sometimes on the cliffs. Yellow-flowered **Wild Cabbage**, an ancestor of Garden Cabbage, grows along the cliffs as far as Old Harry; it is confined to coasts in south-west Britain and blooms in spring. **Wild Parsnip** is also common here and you may find **Pyramidal Orchid** in summer.

Nottingham Catchfly.

Seabirds are visible near the coast path, especially **Herring** and **Great Black-backed Gulls**, which breed here. Some years a hundred or more pairs of **Cormorants** have nested, the largest colony in Dorset. A few **Fulmars** sometimes nest on the cliffs and their effortless, fast, gliding flight distinguishes them from gulls. Other seabirds pass by, the largest being the **Gannet**; adults' white cigar-shaped bodies contrast with their black wing tips and stand out at a distance, with juveniles being browner. **Peregrine** and **Raven** are also frequent here.

Keep well back from the edge of the unstable cliffs. Ballard Down was joined to the Isle of Wight in Palaeolithic times and the rising sea levels and weather combined to erode the chalk connection. The coastal strip along here is known as **Old Nick's Ground** – a reference to the devil. In earlier times, smuggled brandy kegs were hauled up the cliffs and taken over the downs to **Jenny Gould's cottage** on the Swanage–Studland road near the junction leading to Currendon Hill. Parson's Barn was a cave in the cliffs where goods could be stored.

The Pinnacles.

The Pinnacles were created when the cliff base eroded to form a small cave-like hollow, which gradually widened to leave an isolated part. This process is happening all the time and several hollows can be seen here which will form new structures in years to come.

Old Harry Rock guards the north-east corner of Ballard, separated from the nearby **Foreland**. He once had a 'wife', but much of this rock was destroyed in a storm in 1895. Some think the name Harry refers to the devil; a more likely explanation is that the rock was named after notorious 16th-century pirate Harry Paye. The gap between is called **St Lucas's Leap**. There is an old story that a pair of greyhounds belonging to a Studland squire leaped over the cliff while chasing a hare and one of them was named Lucas. A number of ships have been wrecked off Old Harry, including the *San Salvador*; the badly damaged ship had been abandoned by the Spanish Armada and was being crewed by English sailors when it sank in 15 m of water.

The track from Old Harry passes through **Studland Wood**, which contains **Wild Garlic** in spring, its pungent aroma sometimes detected from a distance. **Bluebells, Red Campion** and **Butcher's Broom** are also frequent, while **Orange Tip** butterflies fly along the track. In summer there is a striking patch of **Rose-bay Willowherb**.

Studland Wood.

After the wood the path crosses an open area through fields before passing the northern edge of **Warren Wood**, where a fine **Crab Apple** can be seen in flower from the track in spring. This native species is much rarer than the commonly escaped Apple from gardens, has smaller leaves and is often spiny.

The path now leads into Studland and passes public conveniences near the road. The introduced plant **Himalayan Balsam** grows along the roadside and its pink flowers may be seen in summer. Follow the road to the right. The **Bankes Arms**, location of the Isle of Purbeck Brewery, is just round the corner.

St Nicholas' Church lies a stone's throw away, accessed by a footpath at the north end of the car park. One particularly sad gravestone commemorates three children from the **Marten family** who drowned at Studland; one sibling survived and lived to 92. Late Saxon stonework can be seen in some of the church walls, and the original chancel, nave and central tower would

have dated to this time before later rebuilding. Extensive repairs were made in the late 19th century and excavations showed three distinct levels of grave burial: modern, Saxon Christian and pre-Christian. Other interesting finds include massive red sandstone steps, the keystone of an arch with radius 1.5 m, and two round stones that formed a hand mill. All this provides evidence of a building before the Saxon church, perhaps a Pagan temple as it is known that Christian churches were often built on Pagan sites.

Marten family grave, near the path as you enter the churchyard (north-east end).

The church at Studland.

In 1952 a **Romano-British stone-lined grave** was unearthed in the churchyard and examined by local archaeologist Bernard Calkin. It contained the skeleton of a woman with head and jaw severed and placed near the feet; a shale spindlewhorl and cockle shell were also found. Calkin had previously excavated a cist burial with similar features at Kimmeridge in 1947 (Walk 6). One of the burials at Kimmeridge was late 3rd century, so it is possible the Studland one is contemporary; placing spindlewhorls and shells in graves is evidence of belief in the afterlife and removal of skulls and jaws was presumably done after death as part of some ritual.

Near the porch lies the grave of **Sergeant Lawrence**, a distinguished soldier in the Napoleonic wars, including the Battle of Waterloo, who later came to live in Studland with his French wife. He ran the Duke of Wellington pub, now the Bankes Arms. On the other side of the gravestone his wife's inscription is in French. Above the porch are some **Norman carvings**, including two semi-human figures copulating!

The walk continues south from the church to a crossroads, site of an ancient **Saxon cross**. A restored cross of Saxon design was carved by Purbeck stonemason Trevor Haysom and placed here in 1976.

Two semi-human figures.

Studland Cross.

The road to Glebeland Estate goes through **Manor Farm**. Studland used to form part of the Bankes Estate, which was left to the National Trust in 1981. Glebeland Estate, however, is private and the houses are modern, none of them having numbers. As you climb up the road, look back: older buildings around the church and Manor Farm contrast with the modern homes on the western side of the village.

At the top of the road a gate takes you back onto Ballard Down. Near this gate are several **Buddleias**, which attract many butterflies in late summer. The path to the top of the down is steep, but the view gets more spectacular the higher you climb. Below to the north-west you will see a white-faced building with thatched roof, the settlement of **Woodhouse**. Nearby a number of Romano-British buildings were excavated in the 1950s by Norman Field: several round huts dating from the 1st century and rectangular farm buildings of a later date, with nine Roman coins, including seven from the 3rd century, were found (perhaps the Romano-British grave in Studland churchyard is linked to this settlement?). Eleven fossilised sea urchins were discovered, indicating they had some special significance. Double stalls in two of the later buildings suggest a two-oxen plough team was used. Among other finds were a Kimmeridge shale spindlewhorl and chalk loom weight, which show that weaving was taking place.

When you reach the **oblong stone**, pause to take in the vista. The last part of the walk is westwards along the top of the hill, with panoramic views both sides. As you approach the Obelisk, Agglestone Rock can be seen in the distance on Godlingston Heath, with Poole Harbour and Brownsea Island beyond and Little Sea north-east (Walk 2).

The granite **Obelisk** was erected by George Burt in 1892 to commemorate building the reservoir below to bring clean water to people living in the north of Swanage. It stands adjacent to a Bronze Age **bowl barrow** and both can be seen from miles around. The barrow was excavated by Austen in 1857 and two skeletons were found. The primary burial was at the surprising depth of 4.3 m: a tall man about 1.93 m had been laid in a crouched position and trussed up, indicated by displacement of two vertebrae. A small drinking cup with handle had been placed with him and flint stones carefully laid around the skull and body for protection. He was lying at the bottom of a cist filled with lumps of chalk and pieces of deer antler. The secondary burial, considered to be of a later date, was about 1.2 m below the apex under a stone and consisted of a disunited skeleton, described as being 'very remarkable for size and great breadth'.

Obelisk and Ulwell barrow.

Austen excavated other barrows in Purbeck where evidence of trussed skeletons was found; these Bronze Age burials suggest a belief in the afterlife and possible laying of a ghost. They are also indicative of the foetal position, perhaps the idea being the dead person would be reborn and begin a new life. As with many, if not all, barrows on hillsides, the mounds were constructed to be seen from a distance and likely to have been of prominent people such as tribal chiefs or shamans. The antler in the Ulwell barrow are also of interest: deer were no doubt hunted for food and antler would have been used to help dig the burial mound, but there could also have been a ritual aspect; deer shed their antlers periodically and they are therefore a symbol that life will be renewed: something worn and discarded is replaced with a new form, which is appropriate perhaps for burial of a special person.

Before descending to Ulwell, look west to **Godlingston Hill** with its radio masts. The steep path and steps then take you back to the lay-by. Near the bottom you may see again a profusion of **butterflies** in late summer, attracted to **Marjoram** and **Hemp Agrimony**.

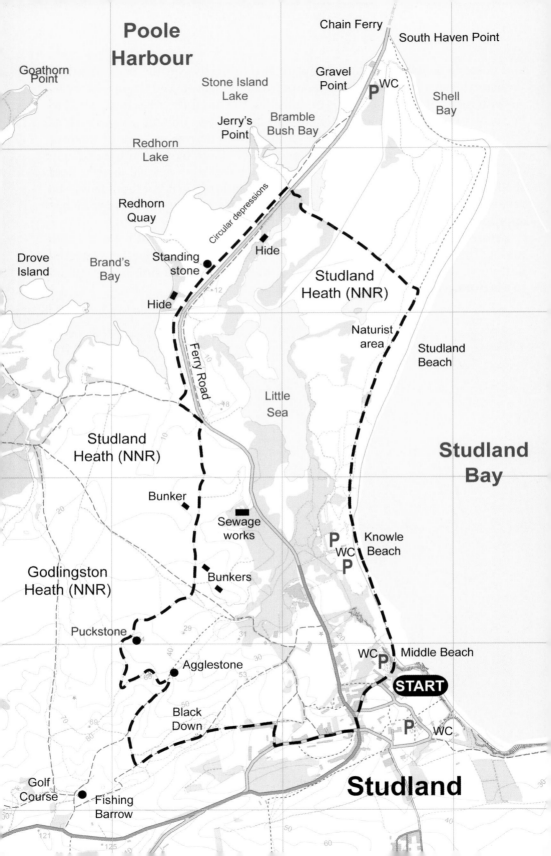

Poole
Harbour

Goathorn
Point

Stone Island
Lake

Chain Ferry

South Haven Point

Gravel
Point

P WC

Shell
Bay

Jerry's
Point

Bramble
Bush Bay

Redhorn
Lake

Circular depressions

Redhorn
Quay

Hide

Drove
Island

Brand's
Bay

Standing
stone

Studland
Heath (NNR)

Hide

Ferry Road

Naturist
area

Studland
Beach

12

Little
Sea

Studland
Heath (NNR)

10

Studland
Bay

Bunker

Sewage
works

8

10

20

Godlingston
Heath (NNR)

Bunkers

P
WC

Knowle
Beach

P

Puckstone

29

31

*

Agglestone

40

53

30

WC P

Middle Beach

Black
Down

50

START

60

69

P WC

70

80

Golf
Course

Fishing
Barrow

Studland

121

125

90

50

60

30

40

Walk 2:
Studland Village to Agglestone Rock, Studland Heath and Beach

Natural features such as the Agglestone and Puckstone, intriguing standing stone and circular marks, heathland flora and fauna and coastal species

Distance: approx. 6 miles, or may be shortened to 3 miles by circling the heath

Best time to do: spring/summer for heathland species, autumn/winter for coastal birds

Refreshments: National Trust café at Middle Beach, Bankes Arms, The Pig (on the beach), Manor Farm Tea Rooms

Parking: Middle Beach or Studland village (SZ 034825)

Suggested route: from Studland village down Heath Green Road and Agglestone Road to access Godlingston Heath, over Studland Heath and back along the beach

Studland is referred to in *Domesday* as 'Stollant', a tract of land where horses are kept. Man's occupation of this area goes back much further as there are a number of prehistoric sites in the area and a Romano-British grave was found in Studland churchyard (Walk 1).

From the village centre walk west down Heath Green Road (opposite Studland Stores), which in spring has typical wayside flowers such as **Alexanders**, **Cow Parsley**, **Greater Stitchwort** and **Herb Robert**. Towards the end of the road, before the turning for Agglestone Road, wiry stems of **Stone Parsley** are evident on the verge in late summer; the plant smells of petrol when crushed.

Turn right into Agglestone Road (unmade surface). Keep walking to the end just past Heath Cottage, where a small gate accesses **Godlingston Heath**. Follow the track in front which skirts south of Black Down. As you head south-west you will notice **heather** species flowering later in summer and some **Holly** bushes, **Pedunculate Oaks**, **Downy Birches** and **Scots Pines** – the latter is not native to the south of England but seeds readily; its orange bark and small cones distinguish it from other pines. To the south the Obelisk and barrow (Walk 1) on Ballard Down stand out, while on your distant right Fishing Barrow (note steps ascending to the summit) and the golf course loom into view.

Fishing Barrow (the name suggests some association with water) is a Bronze Age bell barrow nearly 30 m wide and 2.7 m high, with a well-marked ditch, that has been incorporated into the golf course. There is no record of any excavations, but it is thought that bell barrows, which are round barrows with

33

a platform between the mound and ditch, date to the 'Wessex' Early Bronze Age. As you walk along, note the ironstone that litters the track in places.

Take the prominent right path which skirts the golf course and continue until a slight rise. At the brow of the hill bear right onto a wide path towards the Agglestone. After a short distance there is a magnificent view across the heath, which is home to several special birds, one of which is the **Dartford**

Ironstone.

Warbler. Its scratchy song and furtive flight are diagnostic. Sometimes it will perch on top of a bush, affording a clear view. Unlike most warblers it is present all year and can suffer greatly in severe winters: in the bitter winter of 1962/3 the population was reduced to just a few pairs. Another bird seen most of the year, though some move away in winter, is the **Stonechat**. It is easy to identify with its fondness for perching on bushes, its constantly flicking tail and stone-clinking call; the male is a sprightly bird with black head, white collar and orange-brown underparts.

Two summer visitors to the heath are the Hobby and Nightjar. The **Hobby** is a fast, graceful predator, catching dragonflies and sometimes martins and swallows on the wing; it is a smaller, more scythe-like version of the Peregrine. On warm, still evenings **Nightjars** can be heard churring from dusk onwards, the sound like an old sewing machine. Males also engage in wing clapping when flying and emit a strange croaking call. They can be confiding (approachable) and on occasions will fly close to anyone who has ventured onto the heath at night. Their large gapes are used for scooping up moths. **Glow-worms** may also be found during summer nights, the light emitted by the female beetle to attract a mate being seen from some distance.

Agglestone Rock is a 500-ton natural formation of ferrous sandstone, which is an imposing feature on the landscape. Several legends refer to the rock, one being that the devil threw it from the Isle of Wight at Corfe Castle only for it to fall short. Hutchins suggests the name may derive from Anglo-Saxon 'Halig-stan' meaning 'holy stone' and mentions that country folk referred to it as 'the Devil's Night-Cap'. First reference to it is on Treswell's map of 1586 where the name is 'Adlinston', suggesting 'prince's stone' from 'aedeling' and 'stan'. Whatever the derivation, it is possible that our prehistoric ancestors revered the Agglestone as a place of worship and at certain times of year people may have gone there to perform rituals.

Agglestone Rock.

Bog Asphodel.

In spring, **Gorse** flowers brighten the rather drab appearance of the heath and later in summer **Ling** gives the area a beautiful purple sheen, interspersed with yellow patches of **Dwarf Gorse** that also flowers then. Two other common heathers to look for are pale-mauve **Cross-leaved Heath**, characteristic of wetter areas, and deep-purple **Bell Heather** which prefers drier habitat; both flower June onwards. Wispy patches of **Common Cotton-grass** are seen in wetter areas in summer; these are the seed heads (the flowers are much less conspicuous). Yellow flowers of **Bog Asphodel** (June–July) are also present in some wet areas, followed by the equally prominent orange seed heads.

Take the track south of the Agglestone, first heading west before joining another path that leads north to the **Puckstone**, which is on a small gorse-clad

Godlingston Heath, just east of the Puckstone.

knoll. The rock is formed from the same material as the Agglestone and the name may derive from 'puca stan' ('goblin's stone').

The path continues north-east. After 400 m you cross a more major track. Here you may shorten the walk by turning right and heading back towards Studland across Godlingston Heath. To continue on the described route, head north along the original track. Small **observation bunkers** dotted around the area are relics from WWII. Continue along this track until you see **Little Sea**. This inland lake was created about 400 years ago after sand dunes blocked the connection with the sea and in consequence the water is now fresh. In the late 19th century the lake was partly open to the sea and anyone walking along the beach from Studland to take a boat from the entrance to Poole Harbour had the prospect of wading through water; women were sometimes carried across on the backs of men.

Little Sea.

Good numbers of wintering ducks used to be present, but there has been a huge decline in recent years, thought to have been caused by the introduction of large Carp which have affected the water quality, and many plants have also disappeared. Invasive **New Zealand Pigmyweed** now infests the northern end of Little Sea, and **Pirri-pirri-bur** is taking over many of the sandy tracks around Studland. One welcome species to return is the **Otter** and its increase in Dorset is reflected elsewhere in Britain. **Sika Deer** are often encountered around Little Sea, and the Poole Harbour area is their stronghold in Britain. They were first introduced to Brownsea Island and later swam to the mainland.

The track ends at a gate by Ferry Road. Go through the gate and walk down the narrow unmade road to the left. In early spring aromatic **Bog Myrtle** flowers in boggy areas on the south side of the road. In late summer the roadside is lined with the flowers of **Common Fleabane** and **Hemp Agrimony**, the latter beloved by butterflies.

After about 200 m turn right onto a heathland track (part of Studland Heath National Nature Reserve) and head north again. **Marsh Gentians** can sometimes be seen in wetter areas near the start of this track in late summer/early autumn.

Marsh Gentian. *Silver-studded Blue.*

Two butterflies to look out for are **Silver-studded Blue** (late May–Aug) and Grayling (July–Sept). The former flies low over the heather and takes its name from its underwing patterning, the male's black border to its blue wings helping to distinguish it from other Blues. Its caterpillars feed on heather and gorse and have a close relationship with black ants. The **Grayling** always settles with its wings closed, frequently on tracks to absorb heat, and can be difficult to spot as its underwing colours blend with its surroundings; if you creep up on it, you may observe the beautiful mottled patterning. Its food-plant **Bristle Bent** grows in tufts in dry heath areas. A large green caterpillar found feeding on Ling in summer or crawling over the tracks is likely to be that of the **Emperor Moth**. This is the only British member of the silk-moth family and the caterpillar spins a small cocoon. Adults fly in April/May and males have a highly developed sense of smell to detect females, which produce a lot of pheromones.

Other insects you might see are damselflies and dragonflies; smaller and more delicate damselflies hold their wings above their abdomens, while the faster and more powerful dragonflies hold them at right angles. **Large Red Damselflies**, **Common Blue Damselflies**, **Four-spotted Chasers** and **Common Darters** are the most frequent species encountered. Spiders are most obvious in late summer/ early autumn and a particularly striking one you may see near this track sitting in its web is the **Wasp Spider**. This orb spider takes its name from its coloured pattern; the relatively large black and yellow female is in contrast to the tiny male, which must be careful if it is not to become a meal.

Wasp Spider.

All six species of reptiles can be found on Godlingston and Studland Heaths. The best time to see them is on sunny mornings in early spring, soon after they have emerged from hibernation. **Adders** and **Common Lizards** are most frequently encountered, but the larger **Sand Lizard** (the male is noticeably green in spring) can sometimes be seen in drier areas. The rare **Smooth Snake** spends much of its time underground but may occasionally be found; it has black markings on its body, but not the zig-zag pattern of the Adder, and is a more slender reptile. Its favourite food is lizards, which it catches by coiling its body round its prey and then swallowing it head first. **Slow-worms** (in reality legless lizards) often hide under stones or scrub and can shed their tails if attacked by predators. **Grass Snakes** prefer wetter habitats and can occasionally be seen swimming, including in Little Sea.

As you walk along, **Brand's Bay** comes into view on the left. Birdwatching can be very good here, especially autumn to spring, and a hide can be accessed from the path. The most productive time is on a falling or rising tide when waders such as **Avocets**, **Black-tailed Godwits**, **Greenshanks**, **Common Redshanks**, **Dunlins** and **Grey Plovers** may fly in quite close. **Little Egrets** and **Grey Herons** are sometimes present and often large numbers of duck in winter, especially **Wigeon** and **Teal**. Colourful **Shelduck** can be seen most of the year, and in summer chicks accompany their parents if breeding has been successful.

Brand's Bay.

The path now turns more north-easterly and, after passing several 'crossroads' of tracks, including one on the left that leads to **Brand's Bay hide**, you come to a more prominent east–west path, with the left fork leading to **Redhorn Quay**; on your right is a metal gate by the road. There is a prominent **upright stone** a few metres north-west of the junction of paths (a similar one can be seen on the heath on the other side of the road – see OS map). There used to be a few more, but the others are no longer visible. Their purpose is not clear; they may have been placed here around the time Rempstone Stone Circle (Walk 3) was constructed, about 4000 years ago.

Standing stone on Studland Heath.

They are not the only mystery here: the **ghost of the White Donkey** (see *Paranormal Purbeck – A Study of the Unexplained* by the author) is said to haunt this area of the heath three nights before Christmas. Also, as you continue along the track towards **Jerry's Point** there are a number of **round, shallow depressions** (possibly more than 70 in number) 1.8 m or more across, where the vegetation is different and ground boggier. First recorded in the 19th century, aerial photographs show them more clearly and also an old track that runs through one of them, suggesting a date of some antiquity. Like the standing stones their purpose is unknown, though suggestions include peat cutting or salt pans. Similar circular marks near Stoborough on Holme Heath were excavated by Austen in 1857; he discovered the remains of burnt gorse in a charcoal state and, as there were Bronze Age barrows nearby, speculated that the small mounds might have been used as some kind of ritual funeral pyre.

Circular depression on Studland Heath.

At the track to Jerry's Point turn right and come out by Ferry Road near the bus stop. The walk continues on the path on the other side of the road, heading east to Studland Beach. The start of this track is a good site for dragonflies, including **Downy Emerald** (late May–July) with its gleaming bronze abdomen. The track to the beach goes through an area where naturists may be present.

When you reach the dunes it is best to head for the shore where the going is firmer and then walk back to Studland village. The beach and its low cliffs have suffered erosion over the years and National Trust policy is now to let nature take its course. The sand moves from the south of the bay northwards, where it is contained behind a wall at the mouth of Poole Harbour; with less sand arriving, beaches to the south are shrinking. The dune system is stabilised by plants such as **Marram** and **Lyme-grass**.

Studland Bay is important for wintering birds, and the rare **Black-necked Grebe** can be seen offshore, as well as **Slavonian** and **Great Crested Grebes**. **Great Northern Divers** and **Common Scoters** are sometimes seen offshore and **Red-breasted Mergansers**, **Cormorants** and **Shags** are frequent. **Brent Geese** can be found closer in to shore, where they feed on **Eel-grass**. When the beach is almost deserted in winter, flocks of waders gather, mainly **Dunlins**, **Grey Plovers**, **Ringed Plovers** and **Oyster Catchers**. These species are generally wary of people, but one that is more approachable is the **Sanderling**, a small, pale wader about the size of a Dunlin that dashes along the shore in a frenzy of activity.

Studland Beach is a good place for shells and aptly named **Shell Bay** is just round the corner to the north-west. **Slipper Limpet** was introduced to Britain from North America in the 19th century and the beach can be strewn with thousands of them. Other shells include the **Pod Razor**, **Edible Cockle**, larger **Prickly Cockle**, **Common Mussel**, **Common Whelk**, **Pullet Carpet** and beautiful pink **Thin Tellin**.

Different seaweeds are washed up and come in three colours: green, brown and pink. The appropriately named **Sea Lettuce** is one of the easier green seaweeds to identify, while the long, wide strands of brown **Curvie** are very obvious. Much thinner strands of **Eel-grass** can also be found on the shore; unlike the seaweeds, it is a flowering plant. Two species of **seahorse** occur among the Eel-grass; they are actually small fish with horse-like heads and prehensile tails, which they use to fasten themselves to objects on the seabed. Seahorses may be disturbed by boats anchoring in the Bay, so a voluntary protection zone has been set up.

Old Harry (Walk 1) can be viewed from here. Just before the end of the beach walk up the wooden steps and bear left a few metres, before ascending the path to Middle Beach car park and the village. At the top of the path the **coastguard hut** has display panels on smuggling and shipwrecks. The **wreck of a Spanish merchant ship** carrying pottery and dating from around 1520 was discovered in Studland Bay in 1983 by local divers; some of the objects recovered are in Poole Museum.

Studland Beach erosion.

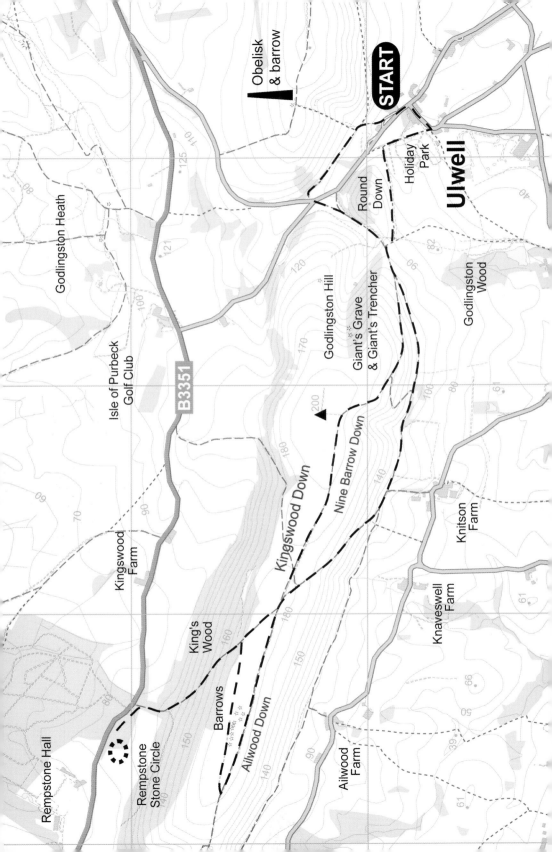

Walk 3:
Ulwell to Ailwood Down, King's Wood and Rempstone Stone Circle

High chalky hills, stunning views, Bronze Age barrow cemetery, Neolithic long barrow, Rempstone Stone Circle and beautiful King's Wood with spring flowers

Distance: approx. 5 miles, or less than 4 miles if not taking in Rempstone

Best time to do: early May for King's Wood; any time for prehistoric features

Refreshments: Village Inn, Ulwell

Parking: in two lay-bys at Ulwell on Studland–Swanage road (SZ 022809)

Suggested route: from Ulwell along Round Down and Godlingston Hill to Knitson, then Nine Barrow Down to Ailwood Down and barrow cemetery. Optional detour down to King's Wood and Rempstone Stone Circle. Return via Nine Barrow Down and Godlingston Hill

From the lay-by take the road to Ulwell Cottage Caravan Park. At the bend enter the Park here and go straight through, heading for the gap in the hills in the far north-east corner. A gate leads onto **Round Down**.

Turn left and clamber a little way up the hill, where you may see more flowers and butterflies and the view is better. The slopes are covered with **Horseshoe Vetch** and **Bird's-foot Trefoil** in late spring/early summer and, like Ballard Down, have good populations of **Adonis Blue** and **Dingy Skipper** butterflies. **Bee Orchids** may occasionally be seen in June/July and **Squinancywort**, **Yellow-wort**, **Wild Thyme**, **Lesser Centaury**, **Harebell** and **Dwarf Thistle** brighten the down in summer, while **Marbled Whites** and **Six-spot Burnet Moths** are obvious in sunshine.

Marbled Whites and Six-spot Burnet Moths on Spear Thistle.

West end of Round Down.

Skirt round the hill to a gap in the chalk; walk through this and follow the Purbeck Way uphill, under the power cable. In the valley below clay-pigeon shooting takes place and there is a Bronze Age bowl barrow near the summit of the facing hill, though not visible from this point. There are two other barrows on Godlingston Hill above – **Giant's Grave** and **Giant's Trencher** – but the area is overgrown with gorse. Both were excavated by Austen, who found nothing, so it is not clear whether they were burial mounds. The names may indicate some folklore. Take the left fork signposted 'Underhill Path'.

Underhill Path.

Godlingston Wood nestles below to the left, from where a spring rises; some of the water is extracted from deep strata and bottled near **Godlingston Manor**, south of the wood. The name may derive from 'Godelin's farm', but there were earlier settlements in the area, as Romano-British pottery and vessels from the Durotriges as well as sling stones have been found south of Godlingston cemetery. The Manor has a tower dating to 1300 and is owned by the National Trust but run as a working farm.

Not many people walk along the bottom path to Knitson, so birds are more likely to be seen here, including **Green Woodpecker**, **Stonechat** and **Yellowhammer**, which are mainly resident. In late summer/early autumn migrant birds such as **Common Redstart** and **Spotted Flycatcher** may be attracted to the trees and bushes, with occasionally a few **Ring Ouzels** in October.

Path above Knitson.

Near the path **Greater Knapweed**, **Hedge Bedstraw**, **Marjoram** and **Restharrow** flower in summer and it is also good for butterflies, with **Lulworth Skipper**, **Essex Skipper**, **Wall** and **Adonis Blue**. An uncommon plant sometimes found is **Henbane**, which has pale yellow flowers netted with purple veins and stickily hairy leaves; it is poisonous and contains alkaloids.

Henbane.

The path to Nine Barrow Down.

After a gate continue on the lower track towards the mobile phone mast. When you reach the pit above Knitson, you will see some farm buildings below. **Knitson**, like Godlingston, had a Romano-British settlement and the present farm is 17th century. Just to the west is Knaveswell Farm. A number of farm settlements were started on the south side of the chalk range to exploit the spring line.

Bear right up the path to **Nine Barrow Down**. Despite its name the barrows are actually on Ailwood Down. In spring you are likely to hear **Skylarks** as you ascend and may see **Buzzards** and **Kestrels**. The honking calls of **Ravens** may also be heard.

Kestrel

At the top of the hill a gate leads onto **Ailwood Down**. Follow the track westwards to the barrows, some of which are visible from the gate. The '**nine barrows**' (in folklore believed to be the burial place of nine kings) are actually 17 Bronze Age bowl barrows. It is recorded that one was opened but only burnt bones were found. There is also a **Neolithic long barrow** immediately south of the round barrows, the only example of its kind in Purbeck and much older (it could date to the early Neolithic). It is over 30 m long, about 12 m wide and up to 1.8 m high. Some Neolithic long barrows were constructed of stone and earth, while others consist of stone chambers; they contain the remains of a number of individuals, often in disarticulated form. Round barrows usually have one or two burials, often in a crouched position, and sometimes grave goods such as pots; cremation was practised at a later date.

After visiting the barrows, go back along Ailwood Down along the wider grassy track. About half-way, at a gap in the trees on the left, a small path leads to some gates. You can take this path into **King's Wood**, down the steep track to Rempstone Stone Circle (and back up again). Alternatively, continue along Ailwood Down. In this north-facing wood, flowers bloom later than elsewhere. Visit in early May for **Bluebells** and a sea of **Wild Garlic**, especially lower

The views from Ailwood Down are some of the best in Purbeck.

Wild Garlic in King's Wood.

down. Other plants include **Wood Anemone, Dog's Mercury, Early Purple Orchid, Greater Stitchwort, Wood Speedwell, Wood Spurge, Primrose, Yellow Archangel** and **Moscatel**.

Some of these species are an indicator that King's Wood may be a relic of ancient woodland (over 500 years old) and there is reference to 'Kyngeswode' as far back as 1397 in the *Calendar of Patent Rolls*. Old **Pedunculate Oak, Hazel** and **Ash** trees attract breeding birds and, as well as resident species, **Willow Warblers, Chiffchaffs** and **Blackcaps** may be heard in spring. **Sika Deer** are sometimes present.

Near the bottom of the wood **Rempstone Hall** may be glimpsed through trees to the north-west; the original 17th-century building was considerably enlarged in the late 18th. On reaching the main road take care. Go left along the verge for about 160 m to **Rempstone Stone Circle** (note the stones are on private land so view them from the verge), consisting of nine stones, several of which have fallen over (others lie scattered in the wood). The stones are made

Rempstone Stone Circle, although very near the road, is quite atmospheric.

of ferrous sandstone from the Bagshot Beds (deposits of clay and sand from about 45 mya, the same material as Agglestone) and form a half circle on the northern side, with a ditch running along the southern flank.

The circle may originally have been about 25 m in diameter and the first reference to it was as recently as 1908. It is thought it may have been erected by the Beaker people in the Early Bronze Age, though no excavations have been carried out. 'Rempstone' may derive from Old English 'Hring-stun' meaning 'ring stone', though there is a reference in 1280 to 'Rameston' which means 'farm where Wild Garlic grows'. In the 1950s two rows of stones were recorded in a field west of the circle, unfortunately later removed by a farmer; it is possible they were part of a processional avenue and that this site was significant in prehistoric times.

Retrace your steps to the top of the wood and the gate accessing Ailwood Down. From here the walk returns to Ulwell via the Purbeck Way over Nine Barrow Down and Godlingston Hill.

Horseshoe Vetch is abundant on lower, south-facing slopes here, which is

Godlingston Hill looking towards Ballard Down.

Yellow-wort.

Common Centaury.

therefore a good site for **Adonis Blues** and **Dingy Skippers**. Another flower of late spring/early summer is **Chalk Milkwort**, with its bright blue petals and white stamens, though the flowers can also be white or pink. Later in summer there is a good display of **Wild Thyme, Yellow-wort, Lady's Bedstraw, Squinancywort, Common Centaury** and **Pyramidal Orchid**.

Once the bottom of the hill is reached, return to Ulwell the same way as before, or continue down Godlingston Hill to the road, cross it and take the footpath back to Ulwell, skirting the bottom of Ballard Down below the Obelisk.

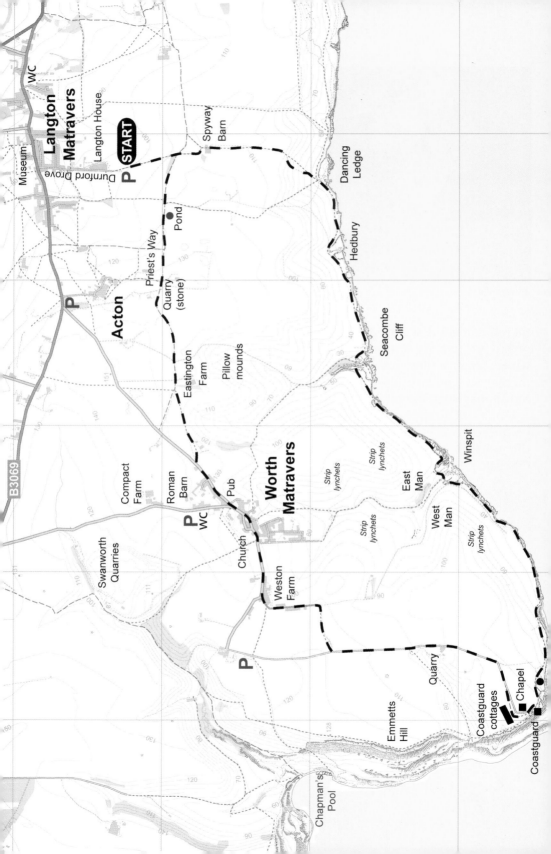

Walk 4:
Langton Matravers to Dancing Ledge, St Aldhelm's Head and Worth Matravers

Spectacular Jurassic Coast scenery, caves and quarries, shipwrecks, an isolated chapel and coastal fauna and flora

Distance: approx. 8 miles

Best time to do: April–September

Refreshments: Worth Matravers Tea and Supper Room, Square and Compass pub

Parking: south end of Durnford Drove past Langton House (SY 997783)

Suggested route: path to Dancing Ledge, then coastal path to St Aldhelm's Head, returning via Worth Matravers and Priest's Way

At the end of Durnford Drove take the footpath south towards Spyway Barn and Dancing Ledge. About 100 m beyond the car park look back towards **Langton House**, an imposing Purbeck stone building now part of the Holiday Property Bond's range of accommodation, built in 1927 by Thomas Pellatt for his daughter Hester.

Langton House. In the distance lies Nine Barrow Down and Godlingston Hill, with Ulwell Gap and Ballard Down north-east.

On the hill almost due north you should be able to make out several **bowl barrows,** part of the so-called nine barrows (actually 17 – see Walk 3); when these barrows were constructed they were clearly meant to be seen from a distance, perhaps as a sign of prestige, territory or religious belief. It is therefore of interest that **Britain's largest Bronze Age axe-head hoard** was discovered east of Langton House in 2007. Four pits containing several hundred axe-heads in pristine condition were found in a field and many other damaged axe-heads were scattered around as a result of ploughing, all Late Bronze Age socketed types. They were freshly cast at the time of burial and unfinished, made of a highly tinned and brittle bronze, giving rise to the view that they were a votive offering to the gods as they would not have been suitable as tools. Two burials dating to around the same period were found in the field, as was a rubbish pit. A field to the south contains a number of small circles where the vegetation is different and consists of sedge, suggesting the soil is wetter and less fertile, possibly evidence of more rubbish pits. A settlement in the Late Bronze Age is therefore possible, though by that time the barrows on the hills to the north would have been hundreds of years old.

The track you are on crosses Priest's Way and continues to **Spyway Barn**. The name originates from a smugglers' look-out. Spyway Farm is owned by the National Trust and consists of 19th-century stone farm buildings. Inside one are displays on local natural history, conservation, quarrying, walking and climbing. Many fields on this walk are bordered by walls of Purbeck stone laid in traditional fashion without mortar.

The path from Spyway continues south towards the sea. **Roe Deer** are sometimes present in fields to the west and in spring and summer you are likely to be serenaded by **Skylarks**, common here. The meadows by the track have **Corky-fruited Water-dropwort** and **Meadow Barley** in summer.

As you reach the top of the hill look down on **Dancing Ledge**. A few pairs of **Puffin** nest on cliffs on the west side and can sometimes be seen flying in and out and also resting on the sea during spring/early summer; binoculars are essential to view them and the best place is near the coast path east of Dancing Ledge where more of the cliff is visible. Puffin breed mainly in the west and north of Britain. **Guillemots** are common breeders here and their torpedo-shaped bodies are a frequent sight. A few pairs of **Razorbills** may also be present; they have blacker bodies than Guillemots and their razor-like bills are shorter than the pointed versions of their close cousins. **Peregrines** are a regular sight and may be seen hunting pigeons, which they strike from the air.

In April/May look out for **Early Spider Orchid** as you descend the hill. The plants are short-lived and half of a population will only flower once or twice, with some entering a

Early Spider Orchid.

dormant phase for a few years. The species is Nationally Scarce (only occurring in Dorset, Sussex and Kent) and Dancing Ledge is one of the best areas in the country to see it, with hundreds of flowers in a good season.

Portland stone quarrying used to take place at **Dancing Ledge** and ruts made by cart wheels in the ledge can be seen from the cliff-top. Stone was unloaded into waiting boats below. Portland stone is much whiter than Purbeck stone and has been used extensively in building work and carving (visit the Langton Matravers and Purbeck Stone Museum to discover more). The stone can be cut or sculpted in any direction without peeling or flaking and was formed from calcium deposits on top of sand grains and shell fragments about 145 mya.

Dancing Ledge takes its name from the wide plateau of limestone just above sea level.

From Dancing Ledge follow the South West Coast Path to Seacombe. The sloping grassland around this area is known as the **Wares**, a Saxon word meaning rough grazing. In spring and early summer **Chalk Milkwort**, **Bird's-foot Trefoil**, **Kidney Vetch**, **Wild Clary** and **Salad Burnet** will be seen along the way close to the path, with **Wild Cabbage** adorning the cliffs. In midsummer you are likely to see **Common** and **Lesser Centaury**, **Yellow-wort**, **Wild Thyme** and **Ox-eye Daisy**, with **Dwarf Thistle** and **Carline Thistle** flowering a little later.

Butterflies include **Marbled White, Wall** and the very local **Adonis Blue** and **Lulworth Skipper**. Look out too for orange **Soldier Beetles** on **Wild Carrot**. There are a few wet flushes among the limestone turf where the vegetation is different from the typical dry habitat.

Between here and Seacombe is an area of cliffs and ledges known as **Hedbury**, named after a local family and not marked on the OS map. Stone was also quarried here and an old cannon can be seen near the cliff edge.

Old Napoleonic cannon on Hedbury cliff.

An introduced species, the **Wall Lizard**, breeds around the cliffs and may occasionally be seen. **Rock Samphire** flowers in late summer, with **Golden Samphire** and **Sea Aster** in smaller quantities. Above Hedbury on the west side is a small colony of **Green-winged Orchids**, including a few albinos, which flower late April–May.

Green-winged Orchid.

The coast path to Seacombe, with strip lynchets above Winspit on West Man.

When you reach **Seacombe Bottom** you will see more evidence of quarrying from the past, though the caves are now closed to the public for safety reasons. Seacombe Bottom was sometimes referred to as Seacombe Gallery, 'gallery' being a local mining term for an underground passage.

The view back towards Seacombe.

Shipwrecks along the Purbeck coast were frequent in times past. The most memorable occurred just west of Seacombe on the night of 6 January 1786. The *Halsewell* was the pride of the East India Company and was sailing from London to Madras with a large number of passengers and goods. She encountered a severe storm near the Isle of Wight and the captain decided to head for Plymouth for urgent repairs. Before they reached Plymouth, however, the wind blew back the ship, which became caught in the infamous Portland

Race and was wrecked on rocks west of Seacombe; 168 people drowned, including Captain Pierce and his two young daughters. The boatswain managed to climb the cliff to raise the alarm, and local quarrymen brought ropes to haul survivors to safety. Eighty-one people were taken to Eastington Farm where they were given soup and dry clothes by Mrs Betty Garland. Once the men had recovered they had to walk back to London and were given a little money by each parish they went through. The East India Company sent 100 guineas for the men who had provided the rescue and a tea-set to Mrs Garland. Victims from the *Halsewell* were buried at Seacombe, but the exact location is not known now.

Scrubby areas around Seacombe can be good for migrant birds such as **Wheatear**, **Whinchat** and **Common Redstart**. **Field Scabious**, **Restharrow** and **Greater Knapweed** grow near the track in summer and the latter is particularly attractive to butterflies and the day-flying **Six-spot Burnet Moth**.

As you approach Winspit, **medieval strip lynchets** on the hill at **West Man** show clearly. These terraces were cut into the hill by the plough to grow crops. The ones at East Man are best seen from the village of Worth Matravers and the two hills together are one of the finest examples in Britain, showing evidence of considerable cultivation (on fairly marginal land) and a relatively high population. There are two types of terraced fields: 'contour scarps' following the contours, and 'up and down' fields which are at right angles to the main slope. Contour scarps are often the most dramatic, with up and down fields frequently destroyed by later cultivation. 'Man' is an old Celtic word for an 'edge promontory of land'.

After the steep steps, as you reach the bottom of the gulley, a small path on the left leads to some old quarry caves; these are home to **Greater Horseshoe Bats**, the largest bat in Britain, now only found in South West England and South Wales.

Bat caves at Winspit.

Winspit Quarry may be worth a detour (but note the quarries and surrounding cliffs are dangerous and you visit at your own risk). Like Seacombe, it has many caves and it was the last of the cliff quarries to close in 1960. Several episodes of *Dr Who* were filmed here. A rare bird, the Wallcreeper, spent the winter of 1969–70 on the cliffs. There is a poignant **memorial stone** to Alastair Ian Campbell Johnstone, a young nature lover who drowned here in 1935.

Unused stone blends with nature beside the path above Winspit Quarry.

Continuing along the coast, more **Wild Cabbage** will be passed on the final stretch to **St Aldhelm's Head**. In some years, the **Blackthorn** may be infested by caterpillars of **Brown-tail Moth** (a tussock moth whose larva has tufts of hair on its back which are incorporated into the silken cocoon) which can strip sections of Blackthorn bare, before spinning cocoons in it to pupate; the caterpillars can reach plague proportions and cause a nasty skin rash, so avoid touching them.

The web of Brown-tail Moth.

As you start to ascend the western side of St Aldhelm's Head, you may see nesting birds such as **Cormorants**, **Herring Gulls**, **Great Black-backed Gulls** and **Fulmars**. On the plateau below are remains of **war-time buildings** related to the development of radar; there is also an **unusually shaped rock** balanced near the cliff-top below the coastguard station. As well as the ubiquitous **Wild Cabbage**, **Greater Knapweed** and **Viper's Bugloss** grow on this plateau.

Rock left by quarrymen as a warning of the dangerous currents offshore.

Just before the coastguard station is a **memorial to the radar scientists** who worked here during WWII. Nearby are displays about the secret **Telecommunications Research Establishment** set up in 1940 when a radar station was built to search for German bombers flying at very low level across the Channel; it was a major contribution to winning the war, and for 2 years over 2000 people were employed in laboratories and workshops here.

The **coastguard station** has commanding views of the Channel and is worth a visit to learn about the valuable work that it provides. It is manned by watch-keepers every day of the year except Christmas Day. The sea chart inside

Coastguard Station on St Aldhelm's Head.

shows St Aldhelm's Ledge stretching 4 miles into the Channel; the depth of water varies considerably on either side and this can cause problems to shipping. There is usually a welcome water bowl here for dogs.

Walk a little further west and you will be treated to magnificent views of the coast towards Chapman's Pool, Houns-tout, Kimmeridge, Gad Cliff and Worbarrow Bay. Across the sea, Portland may be discernible in the distance.

The **'chapel'** at St Aldhelm's Head is a curious building and its original function is controversial. The solid central pillar inside and roof vaulting are reminiscent of an ecclesiastical foundation, yet the building has no east–west alignment (as churches and chapels have) but faces the four compass points, and the two slit windows (one now bricked over) seem designed to look out on the Channel. The central pillar in fact would have obscured the view of any altar to some of the congregation and the cross on top of the building was

placed there in 1874. Many dates (1665, 1689, etc.) have been carved into the pillar and hairpins were placed in the joints to make wishes; even sheep were kept in here at one time. It has been

Twelfth-century St Aldhelm's chapel.

suggested that the building could have acted as a watch tower (the date may be contemporary with the keep at Corfe Castle at the time of the civil war during King Stephen's reign), but there is no trace of any steps leading to the top of the building. It is recorded that in the 13th century St Aldhelm's Chapel was served by a royal chaplain. It stands on a raised platform in the middle of an irregular earthwork enclosure and there may well have been other buildings here. Celtic fields, sometimes overlain by strip fields, cover an area of about 25 ha north and north-east of here.

Approximately a quarter of a mile NNE an **interesting grave** was unearthed by the plough in 1957. It consisted of a Purbeck Marble coffin lid, underneath which was the skeleton of a woman. Near the grave was a small square stone foundation and it is thought that the woman might have lived there as an anchoress (female holy hermit). Her grave was dated to between 1250 and 1275 and she was clearly someone of importance. Was she in some way connected with the chapel?

From here follow the rough road (bridleway) past St Aldhelm's Head quarry. In summer **Common Red Poppy**, **Greater Knapweed** and **Stinking Chamomile** may line the road. **Skylarks** are much in evidence in spring and near the quarry you may see **Yellowhammers**. If lucky you might hear the call of a **Corn Bunting**, which sounds like a bunch of jangling keys. The species has declined in recent years but may still breed in this area. It is quite drab in appearance and on account of this was sometimes referred to as 'the fat brown bird of the barley'; its diagnostic call and fondness for perching on posts make it easy to spot.

St Aldhelm's Head quarry.

On the ridge just east of the quarry, pottery sherds, the earliest believed to be Early Iron Age, and later Samian and Romano-British coarse ware, have been found, together with a coin of Gallienus (253–268 CE) and five lathe-turned shale armlet cores.

Continue along the narrow road until you come to a crossing of tracks. Take the right-hand path marked 'Worth ¾'. Follow the track round to **Weston Farm** and turn right at the main road to reach the main part of **Worth Matravers** village. Early Iron Age pottery sherds have also been found at Weston Farm, in addition to Romano-British sherds and worked shale. In *Domesday* Worth is spelled variously 'Orde', 'Wirde', etc. meaning 'enclosure'. The area still shows signs of the typical medieval settlement pattern in Purbeck consisting of small hamlets and farms, each set out in an approximately rectangular area of land bounded by stone walls and hedges. In spring yellow-green flowers of **Alexanders**, which are attractive to insects, adorn the roadside; it is quite a common plant in Purbeck and was formerly used as a remedy for flatulence.

Attractive chancel arch inside the church.

The **church of St Nicholas of Myra** is passed as you walk through the village. The main body dates to around 1100, so it is early Norman. Just inside the porch is the **Purbeck Marble coffin lid** belonging to the 'anchoress' found near St Aldhelm's Head. When you enter the church itself, turn round and look up at the mirror hanging above the door; this came from the wreck of the *Halsewell* and belonged to one of the ladies who drowned.

In the churchyard on the north side lies the tomb of **Benjamin Jesty** and his wife. Jesty, who was a tenant farmer at nearby Downshay Farm, was the pioneer of smallpox vaccination and experimented on his wife and children by successfully inoculating them with cowpox.

Continue through the village to the **duck pond**, with the **Square and Compass pub** further on, from where you can enjoy good views of the **strip**

Jesty graves in the churchyard.

lynchets on East and West Man. The strips range from 70 to 280 m long and some of the riser heights are up to 4.5 m.

The pub has been run by the Newman family for over 100 years and a local book has been produced on its history and characters. An interesting **museum** inside contains a collection of prehistoric tools (some found locally), coins, jewellery and pottery, evidence that there were **ancient settlements in the area** over a long period, reinforced by excavations north of the pub and south of Compact Farm, where remains dating from many periods have been found. In the 1990s some Early Iron Age remains were found and evidence of further occupation in the Late Iron Age/Early Romano-British period, with two round houses and a later rectangular building that was then replaced by another which included a grain-drying oven. A large number of pottery sherds were recovered (some from Gaul, Spain and Italy), together with shale armlets (see Walk 6 for details of this industry); a stylus and inkwell suggest some degree of literacy. The highest number of animal bones were sheep, though there was no evidence of cloth making.

The Square and Compass museum contains fossilised dinosaur bones, crocodile teeth and turtle remains, among other exhibits.

Two Durotrigan burials of crouched older men were discovered: one inside one of the round houses suggests the grave postdated the house, the first example of an adult burial within a round house (which was not normally the custom). The second unusual feature is that one grave appeared to be the mirror image of the other, with the burial inside being north-west of the entrance and the skull at the west end of the grave, while the other grave was outside and south-east of the entrance with the skull at the east end.

Highlights of later excavations included a Neolithic ditch, two rows of small stone slabs from the Early Bronze Age (2200 BCE), post pits of a Late Bronze Age round house (900–800 BCE), a large cobbled area used as a meeting place (800–700 BCE) for trade and celebrations, and a piece of glass from *c* 600 BCE (the oldest known glass in Dorset). Additionally, 17–18 infant burials from the Roman period, perhaps evidence of infanticide, sometimes practised at this time, and a Post-Romano cemetery were discovered. The site has now become an affordable housing development and is appropriately named Roman Barn.

From the pub, walk up the road until you come to a footpath to Swanage. Head east across three fields, where there is a signpost to Langton Matravers 1½ miles. **Priest's Way** is the track the priest from Worth followed in medieval times to Swanage to take services; in those days the church at Worth was more important than the one at Swanage, which was actually included in the parish of Worth until *c* 1500.

Signs for Priest's Way.

Eastington Farm on the right belonged to Christchurch Priory in the medieval period, clearly showing the extent of the power of the church at that time. Just south of Eastington are remains of a medieval settlement and three pillow mounds (marked on the OS map), perhaps related to medieval rabbit warrens.

Eastington Farm from Priest's Way.

Along the way you will pass **piles of stone** that have been quarried and are awaiting transportation. The stone industry is of great importance in the history of Purbeck and, although many quarries have now closed, a few opencast are still working.

The pond on your right has the introduced yellow-flowering **Fringed Water-lily** (July–Sept) and also the scarce **Narrow-leaved Bird's-foot Trefoil** which flowers in late summer. Soon after you will see **Spyway Barn** in the distance and can then follow either footpath back to **Durnford Drove**.

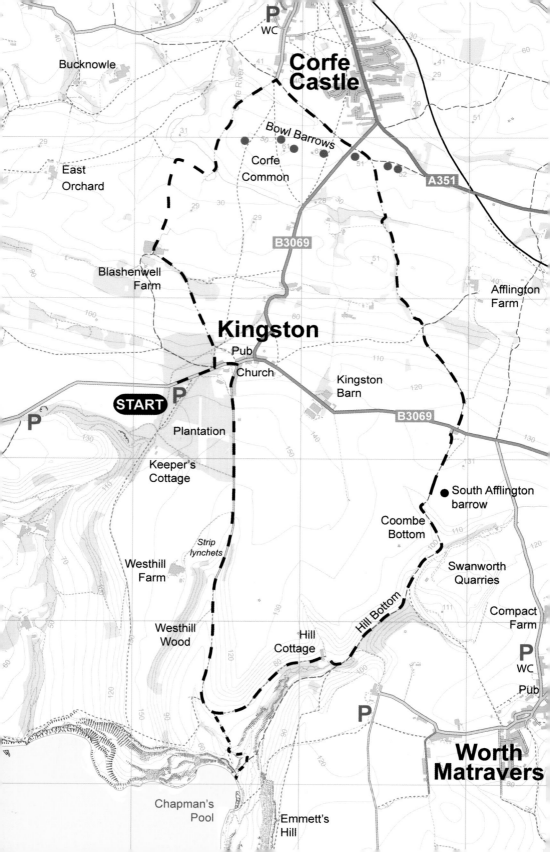

Walk 5:
Kingston to Corfe Common, Hill Bottom and Chapman's Pool

Purbeck Marble, prehistoric finds near Blashenwell, rich flora of Corfe Common and scenic Chapman's Pool

Distance: approx. 7 miles, with an extra mile to fully explore Chapman's Pool

Best time to do: May–September

Refreshments: Scott Arms, Kingston

Parking: The Plantation (Houns-tout) car park (SY 954795)

Suggested route: Kingston to Corfe Common via Blashenwell Farm, join the Purbeck Way to Kingston Road, continuing to Coombe Bottom, Hill Bottom, Chapman's Pool and back to Kingston

Purbeck Marble is a form of Purbeck Stone consisting of the fossilised remains of tiny snails and when polished is usually bluish-grey. The rock is exposed at Peveril Point, Swanage, and continues as a narrow seam west to Worbarrow Bay. The Romans were probably first to exploit it, for memorials, wall inlays and mouldings, but found it was not suitable for outdoor purposes as it weathers badly. During the Middle Ages it was used extensively inside churches and cathedrals for piers, pillars and tombs. West Street in Corfe Castle, where the stone was worked, became the centre of the industry. The stone was quarried at sites such as Wilkswood, Quarr, Dunshay and Afflington and then transported by cart to Corfe.

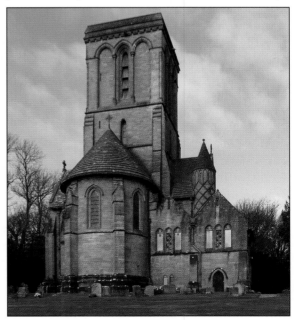

Walk down the road from the Plantation to **St James's Church** (at the west end of Kingston), which has some

St James's Church, Kingston.

67

fine Purbeck Marble pillars inside (see photo in 'Purbeck Through History' chapter). The church was built in the 19th century by the 3rd Earl of Eldon who owned Encombe Estate surrounding Kingston. St James's was intended as a private church for the Earl's family and its construction saw the last major use of Purbeck Marble. The older church at the east end of the village (near the bus stop) is now a private house, but for a time this small village had two churches. In *Domesday* Kingston is referred to as 'Chingestone' meaning 'king's farm', originating in Saxon times, but in 948 King Eadred granted the land to the Abbess of Shaftesbury.

At the north-west end of the churchyard is a footpath sign across the road almost opposite; take the right-hand fork and head down through the wood in a northerly direction, passing **Wild Garlic** and **Lesser Periwinkle** in spring. The path joins the main woodland track for a few metres and then bears left a short way before reaching a stile.

Over the stile, cross the field in a north-westerly direction. Birds of prey such as **Buzzards**, **Kestrels** and **Peregrines** can be frequent here.

The track continues through scrub until you come to **Blashenwell Farm**. Go into the farmyard and bear right past a waterwheel and lovely pond. The house is late 18th century, but there is a much older history at Blashenwell as this is one of only two sites in Purbeck with evidence of a **temporary Mesolithic camp**: two tranchet axes, three microliths and a number of sea shells have been found and the natural spring nearby no doubt encouraged settlement. In 1965 a tightly contracted inhumation burial, possibly Early Bronze Age, was unearthed between two slabs of stone. Other discoveries included floors of paving stones, traces of hearths and shale armlet core waste (see Walk 6 for details of this industry at Kimmeridge) dating from the Early Iron Age to the

Old water wheel at Blashenwell Farm.

Roman period, showing that the site was popular at many different periods. The earliest reference to Blashenwell is in 955 in the *Shaftesbury Register* where it is referred to as 'Blechenhamwelle', suggesting a place where cloth was bleached, from 'blaecen' meaning 'bleaching'.

Leaving Blashenwell, head along the road towards Corfe Castle. **Creech Barrow Hill**, one of the highest points in Purbeck, stands out clearly on the ridge top. Closer and more to the north-west are several buildings forming the settlement of Bucknowle. Between Bucknowle and Corfe Castle a **Roman villa** was discovered in 1975, one of three in the area. During excavations seven distinct periods from the Iron Age to Late Roman were identified and a tessellated floor found. Shale furniture was produced in the villa's workshops and good quality pottery was used, showing the family were high status. There are photographs of some of the finds in the New Inn, Church Knowle, with Roman pottery and flue tiles in Corfe Castle Town Trust Museum. On the highest point of Corfe Common, overlooking Bucknowle, both **Durotrigan and Roman coins** have been found and also wall foundations, which may indicate a possible temple site; the Durotrigan coins had a high silver content so may date to around 50 BCE, while the Roman ones date up to the late 4th century.

After crossing a cattle grid follow the road to the north end of the common, or walk on the common within sight of the road and look at some of the plants. Much of **Corfe Common** consists of damp neutral (neither too acidic nor too alkaline) grassland, with some very wet areas, and it has a rich flora. In spring it is carpeted with **Bluebells**, and other frequent species include **Lousewort, Lady's Smock, English Eyebright** and **Tormentil. Heath Spotted Orchids** can be quite common in early summer and later **Betony, Fleabane, Golden-rod, Harebell, Saw-wort** and **Devil's-bit Scabious** form a patchwork of colour. **Yellowhammers** are present here and **Buzzards** may be soaring overhead.

Golden-rod.

Saw-wort.

At the fences and gates bear right. This **old cart track** was used to transport Purbeck Marble, as previously mentioned. Near the start there are sometimes a few **Green-winged Orchids** (named from the veins on the hood above the flower) in spring. **Chamomile** occurs in some of the short grassland and flowers

View of Corfe Castle from the Common.

later in summer; it was sometimes used in lawns and has a pungent scent when crushed. A native species, it is now quite scarce.

Chamomile.

Take the lower route, aiming to the right of the last house in front. On reaching the marker post you join the **Purbeck Way**. Note several **Bronze Age bowl barrows** on the ridge to your right; well-preserved examples of **Celtic fields** occur on the other side of the ridge. As you approach the gate look out for **Southern Marsh Orchids** (May–July) on the left in wetter areas. Providing they have not been grazed by horses, their tall pink spikes can

Corfe Common.

show well; the leaves are not spotted, but there are hybrids with Heath Spotted Orchid.

Cross the road and continue on. At the start of the track, about 20 m east of the gate, there may be a fine display of **Heath Dog-violets** (note the yellow spurs) in early May. You will see several Bronze Age **bowl barrows** on the hillock ahead.

Head SSE by the stone marker, down the hill. Follow the sign to Chapman's Pool and exit the common over a plank bridge, after which you enter a field. Here on, follow the Purbeck Way. As you climb higher, **Afflington Farm**, part of which dates to the early 17th century, comes into view on the left. This is one site where Purbeck Marble was quarried and in the 13th century it even had its own market and fair.

After a gate near some large stones bear left for a short distance before heading SSE again. As you go up the track, look back for a magnificent view of **Corfe gap** (the name 'Corfe' means 'gap' or 'cutting').

On reaching the main road, **Kingston Barn** is on your right in the distance. In 1960 a **Roman Pagan altar** of Purbeck Marble was found nearby, of rough workmanship and uninscribed, with a concave circle on top into which a libation of wine would have been poured. As it is only just over a metre in height, it would have been portable and may have been used by Roman soldiers. It is possible there was a small temple, and the few large stones found nearby may indicate some kind of structure. Samian (reddish-brown fine-ware pottery imported from France and Germany) and coarse-ware pottery sherds from the Roman period as well as shale fragments have been recovered.

Cross the road and follow the sign to Chapman's Pool between two buildings. Just before reaching **Coombe Bottom**, there is a bowl barrow in the field to your left. Known as **South Afflington barrow** it was excavated by Austen in the 19th century. He found a probable primary cremation with a shale ring covered by a large urn, and also a grave containing a crouched interment. Nearer the surface were nine skeletons in two parallel rows of three and four graves, some of which were stone-lined; a bronze ring was found in one grave, and what may have been bronze strap-fittings and a stud had been placed in the upper part of the barrow. These nine skeletons of a later date are believed to be Romano-British.

Swanworth Quarries lies south-east, one of several open-cast quarries in the area supplying aggregate from limestone and chert (a type of quartz resembling flint). **Compact Farm** is beyond the quarry and a number of historical remains have been found south of the farm (Walk 4).

The path goes down through **Coombe Bottom** and continues round into **Hill Bottom**. These sheltered areas act as sun traps and are favoured by butterflies, some of which are attracted by the **Buddleias** which flower later in summer. There are plenty of trees and scrub for birds to shelter and nest in, and flowers such as **Cow Parsley** and **Red Campion** can be found along the way, with **Old Man's Beard** from late summer onwards.

Coombe Bottom, awash with Old Man's Beard.

Emmetts Hill and Chapman's Pool.

Sheep in field above Chapman's Pool.

Emerge onto a narrow road and follow the sign to Chapman's Pool. Soon after you will reach another sign; continue on the Kimmeridge route. Pass Hill Bottom Cottage, followed by the coastal path to Houns-tout, and walk down this track. Nearing the coast the view opens up, with **Chapman's Pool** before you, **Emmetts Hill** to the left and **Houns-tout** right.

At the tarmac road you can detour to Chapman's Pool, but you may find the beach closed due to landslips and cliff falls and the steep path down to the Pool quite challenging. The cliffs are composed of **Kimmeridge Clay** and the old boat hut is visible from a distance. There is a reference to Chapman's Pool as far back as 948 and the name may refer to a pool that is short in extent and which is in common use, from 'mannes' meaning 'community'; in fact the Pool lies in two parishes, Corfe and Worth.

Houns-tout from Chapman's Pool.

In fields along the road back to Kingston sheep-farming is evident. On the left lies narrow Westhill Wood, above which some Romano-British pottery was found and also clay roof-tile fragments, flint flakes and shale waste.

After the cattle grid, on the left is a good example of some **medieval strip lynchets**. On the other side of the road two **prehistoric or Romano-British settlements** were found within an ancient field system, with several hut circles and pottery sherds discovered.

Before reaching Kingston you pass the east end of **the Plantation**, where **Wild Garlic** and **Cow Parsley** look beautiful in spring.

Westhill Wood and Cottage.

The Plantation (opposite page).

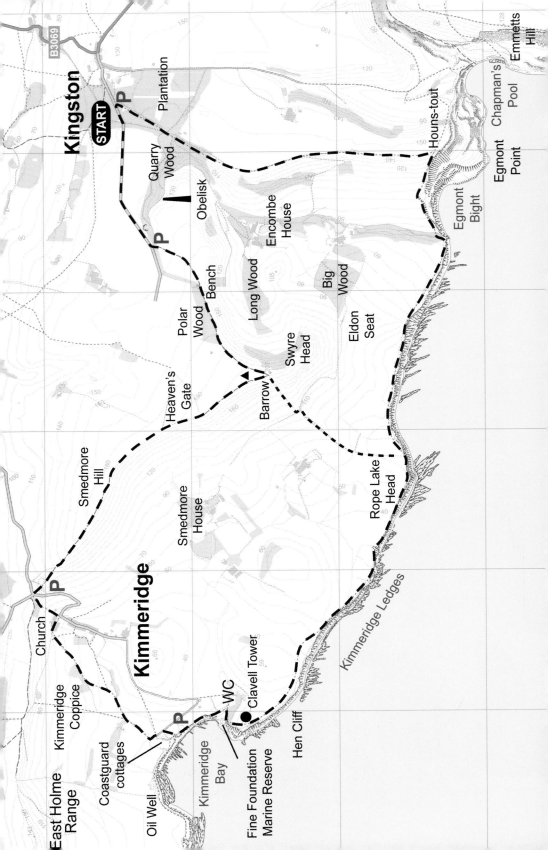

Walk 6:
Kingston to Kimmeridge and Houns-tout

Prehistoric sites, highest point in Purbeck, marine reserve at Kimmeridge, Clavell Tower and stunning views

Distance: approx. 10 miles, but route can be shortened by approx. 1.5 miles at Rope Lake Head

Best time to do: spring to autumn

Refreshments: Clavell's Cafe and Restaurant, Kimmeridge; Scott Arms, Kingston

Parking: the Plantation (Houns-tout) car park (SY 953795)

Suggested route: out to Swyre Head, along Smedmore Hill, through fields to Kimmeridge; return by coastal path to Rope Lake Head, and on to Houns-tout and Kingston

If starting from the bus stop in Kingston, proceed west along the road past the Scott Arms and church (Walk 5). Continue in the same direction when you reach **the Plantation** and first car park. As its name implies, the woodland consists of many planted trees, though orchids including **Twayblade** and **Greater Butterfly** can be found on some of the verges. The road soon emerges from the wood into open fields; a number of interesting plants grow at the field edge on the left, including rare **Broad-leaved Spurge**.

Continue along to Sheep Pens car park. Bear left here and follow the sign to Swyre Head. You will come out onto downland, with **Polar Wood** on the right, consisting of mainly **Ash** and **Sycamore** with a mass of **Bluebells** in spring. The sound of **Skylarks** fills the air in spring and it is a good location to see birds of prey such as **Buzzards**.

Looking towards Swyre Head, with 'Golden Bowl' valley to the left.

77

Polar Wood in spring-time.

The valley below ('the Golden Bowl') contains **Encombe House**, partly obscured by trees, rebuilt by politician John Pitt in the 18th century and later home of the Earls of Eldon (Scott family). An artificially created lake is also visible and most of the trees near the house were planted. Encombe – with

RAF memorial bench.

first reference in 1244 to 'Hen(n) ecumbe' – literally means 'Hens' valley'.

You will pass a seat, a memorial to those killed in two RAF flying accidents nearby: in 1938 three men died in a training flight crash and in 1945 an RAF Liberator came down following loss of fuel pressure, resulting in 27 deaths and making it Dorset's worst-ever air crash.

The view back along Polar Wood.

Walk along the top of the hill to **Swyre Head** ('Swira' is West Saxon for 'hill' or 'ridge') with its Bronze Age **bowl barrow**. There is a magnificent view westwards from the barrow, which is the highest point in Purbeck. Just below in the valley to the west lies **Smedmore House**. Built by Sir William Clavell at the beginning of the 17th century and considerably remodelled in the 18th, it is open to the public two weekends a year in aid of local charities.

Bowl barrow on Swyre Head.

Golden-ringed Dragonflies mating.

From the barrow head north-west to a gate leading to a track along the top of **Smedmore Hill**. Through the gate, look north-east to obtain a splendid view of **Corfe gap**. Next is **Heaven's Gate**, no doubt because of the fine views again. **Hares** and **Red-legged Partridges** may be present in fields here, and look out for **migrant butterflies** and local **Golden-ringed Dragonflies**. A probable

View from Swyre Head.

prehistoric or Romano-British settlement was discovered on the north slope of Smedmore Hill, with platformed enclosures and some Iron Age and Romano-British pottery.

As the track descends, you will see **Blackmanston Farm** and **Steeple church** in the distance; about half a mile north-west of the church is a small coppice by the name of **Hasler**, where Hasler Hundred court met in Late Saxon times (Purbeck was divided into two 'hundreds' at this time for local administration).

As the track nearly reaches the road, it passes a disused quarry (overgrown) on the left, close to which nine or ten **cist burials** were found; at least some were of shale and the burials may have been Romano-British.

Narrow-leaved Everlasting-pea.

At the road turn left. On the other side, almost opposite the track you have just left, grows the tall and uncommon **Narrow-leaved Everlasting-pea**; its pink flowers can be admired in summer.

Walk down the road a few metres to the junction and follow the sign to Kimmeridge, descending towards the village. In *Domesday* **Kimmeridge** is referred to as 'Cameric', which probably means a 'convenient or splendid strip of land, stream or narrow road' from the words 'cyme' and 'ric', perhaps referring to the track running from Smedmore Hill down to Kimmeridge Bay. In medieval times there were three settlements in the parish: Kimmeridge, Smedmore and Little Kimmeridge, each of which had a rectangular parcel of land stretching from the sea to Smedmore Hill; the old boundaries are preserved as continuous hedge lines. The modern village contains houses dating to the 17th century.

The **church** was rebuilt in the 19th century, though traces of older history remain including Norman arches above the porch. On the west side of the churchyard is a line of **coastguard graves**; some of the men died as a result of tragic accidents.

Leaving the church, go down to the road and turn right onto a track signposted Kimmeridge Bay. Take the lower path across fields, heading south, towards the coastguard cottages in the distance.

At the end of the copse follow the green footpath sign left towards Clavell Tower. Skirt round the fields to the road.

Turn left at the road and walk to the car park area above the bay and view the display boards. A few metres west of these, some steps lead down to the beach. The **pill box** and **dragon's teeth** are leftover war-time defences. Turn left and walk along the beach to the Marine Centre, or if the tide is high take the cliff-top path. From the beach there is a good perspective of the different layers of clay and shale that form **Kimmeridge Clay**. These rocks were laid down 155 mya on the floor of a deep tropical sea and are famous for **fossil ammonites, reptiles and fish**. Note that loose fossils may be collected from the beach, but hammering for fossils in the crumbling cliffs is forbidden. The rocks here have been folded into a dome-like structure which acts as a trap for oil, rising from older rocks deep underground. The **nodding donkey** at the western end of the bay has been pumping oil since its discovery by BP in 1959.

Kimmeridge Bay.

A much older industry at Kimmeridge was that of **shale**, used in the manufacture of **armlets** (rings worn around the arms) in the Early Iron Age and later Romano-British period, and a workshop was found here; the large

Kimmeridge cliffs and beach.

amount of shale waste core and specialised flint tools suggest the later industry was lathe turned. During the process of producing armlets, the central core of shale was removed and in the 19th century it was believed that these disc-shaped objects were ancient coins, so they became known as '**Kimmeridge pennies**'. Shale was also used to make **spindlewhorls**, which acted as weights on the spindle to help it rotate more easily when spinning wool. **Salt boiling** also took place from the Early Iron Age, and fragments of jars consisting of coarse reddish clay probably associated with the industry have been discovered. **Sling stones** (in the form of beach pebbles) have been found and an intriguing **pentagonal cist** consisting of shale slabs containing a possible bullock sacrifice.

In 1947 archaeologist Bernard Calkin excavated an **unusual cist burial** on the cliffs here and found the skeletons of two elderly women. In the primary burial the skull and jaw had been placed near the knees, and in the secondary the lower jaw lay near the knees. Shale spindlewhorls accompanied the burials and limpet and snail shells had been placed with the primary interment. A coin of Emperor Carausius dated the primary burial to the late 3rd century. (See Walk 1 for a similar burial at Studland.)

At low tide some of the marine life near the ledges may be evident, the most obvious being **limpets**, **top shells**, **winkles**, **barnacles**, **Beadlet Anemones**, and **seaweeds** (a number of rare seaweeds occur here), and **Blennies** and **Shore Crabs** in the rock pools. A 400-m-long snorkel trail offers an introduction to the wildlife found here. Fish include **Pollock**, **Mullet** and **Corkwing Wrasse**, while **Snakelocks Anemones** and pink **Coral Weed** abound. Beneath the rocky ledge, **prawns**, **crabs**, **Fan Worms** and **fish** hide among the caves and fissures.

The Fine Foundation Marine Centre was established in 1978 by Dorset Wildlife Trust as Britain's first voluntary marine reserve. It has free admission and toilets. The Purbeck coast is internationally important for its marine wildlife and habitats. Displays include a small aquarium, a remotely controlled seabed camera, dolphin skulls, fossil ammonites, shells and information on local fishing and coastal litter. There is a fossil Plesiosaur rib showing bite marks from what may have been a crocodile. Outside is the skull of a **Fin Whale**, the second largest mammal in the world (after the Blue Whale); its body was washed up nearby in 2012, the first to be found in Dorset.

After visiting the Centre, return to the road and follow the sign to **Chapman's Pool** up steps. At the top is **Clavell Tower** and nearby you will see

Clavell Tower.

its original circular base close to the cliff; the tower was moved away from the crumbling edge in 2008. The three-storey brick and rubble edifice was built as a folly in 1831 by Rev John Richards, who took the name Clavell as a condition of inheriting Smedmore Estate. Its height and prominent location ensured it became a coastguard lookout. It features in P.G. James' novel *The Dark Tower* and is now looked after by the Landmark Trust and used for holidays.

The South West Coast Path now takes you along **Hen Cliff** towards **Rope Lake Head**. You will pass a lot of **Wild Cabbage** and also some **Black Mustard**. This is a good area for **Peregrines** as well as passing migrant birds. The cliffs along this route suffer from landslips and there may be path detours. In the 19th century tramways in connection with mineral extraction were constructed along here.

View west towards Gad Cliff and Worbarrow Tout.

Remains of old tram track on Hen Cliff.

Near Rope Lake Head a **settlement site** was discovered with evidence of occupation from the Late Bronze/Early Iron Age to Roman times, with one coin dating to the 4th century. Shale and salt production were important here and a field system was developed.

Just after Rope Lake Head you may take the permissive path to Swyre Head to shorten the walk, or carry on to Houns-tout. An area near the cliff edge here has been disturbed by **Badgers** and **Rabbits**, where there is a good population of **Bur Chervil** and some **Milk Thistle**. **Wall** butterflies frequent this stretch of coast.

After ascending a small steep hill, on the left is a gate marked 'Private, No Access'; north of this on the hillside above is the stone **Eldon Seat**, erected by the 1st Earl of Eldon to provide a view over his house and lake. A **settlement** was found at Eldon Seat and, like the one near Rope Lake Head, was in use around the same time and extended to the cliff edge. The site was excavated by Professor Barry Cunliffe in the 1960s and found to be associated with the manufacture of shale armlets. Some of the bucket and barrel-shaped urns found derive from local Bronze Age forms and may be 8th century BCE. Four round houses were found, two of which had large central hearths, and it is possible that leather production took place, as bone awls and rib knives were discovered. A field system was also developed and by the 6th century BCE sheep had become more prevalent than cattle, a trend apparent elsewhere in Wessex.

View to Houns-tout and St Aldhelm's Head.

The path now descends to **Egmont Bight**, where there is a lovely display of **Wild Garlic** in spring, before making the steep ascent to **Houns-tout**. The name may mean 'look-out hill' and it is certainly a good vantage point as, once you reach the top, there is a magnificent view westwards. A Purbeck Marble **mortarium** (small Roman bowl for mixing herbs and spices) was found on the cliff edge here and can be seen in the Langton Matravers and Purbeck Stone Museum.

From the top of Houns-tout follow the track northwards back to Kingston. You will see **Encombe House**, lake and estate buildings below to your left and, then, as you near the wood, a stone **obelisk**, erected for a member of the Scott family. About 460 m west of the obelisk, a rectangular building, which had probably been thatched, and shale armlet waste were excavated in 1954; pottery sherds from the Roman period as well as the Early Iron Age were also found.

View from Houns-tout, with Egmont Bight below and Swyre Head top right.

The track leaves the down to enter **Quarry Wood**. During quarrying in the late 18th century a **skeleton**, placed under two large flat stones positioned edgeways, was found here, together with a large vessel full of shale armlet cores – yet more evidence of this early industry in Purbeck. Continue through the Plantation back to Kingston.

Encombe House.

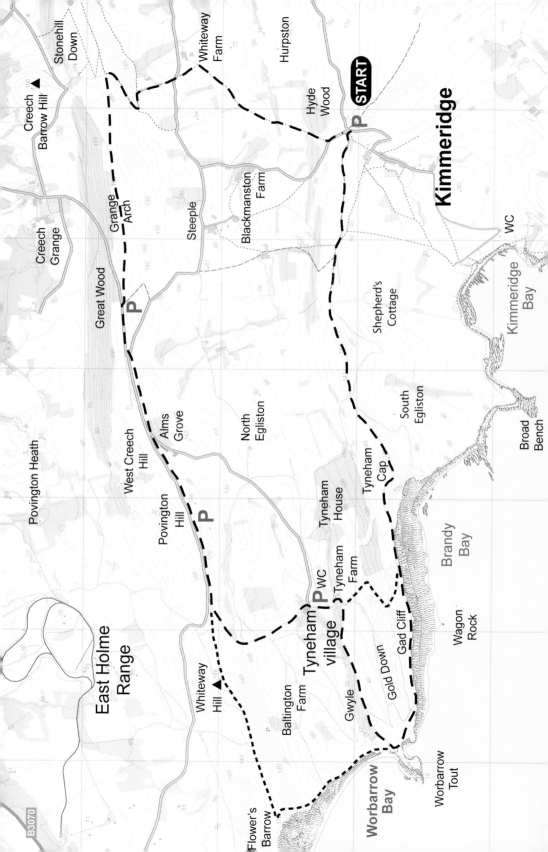

Walk 7:
Kimmeridge to Tyneham and Grange Arch

Dramatic coastal scenery, 'ghost' village of Tyneham,
Flower's Barrow hill fort and ridgeway path along the hill-top

Distance: approx. 10 miles

Best time to do: spring to autumn, but check opening times of Lulworth Ranges (normally open at weekends and holidays)

Refreshments: Clavell's Cafe and Restaurant, Kimmeridge

Parking: unnamed car park NE of Kimmeridge in an old quarry, just over ridge after signs to B&Bs (SY 918800)

Suggested route: north of Kimmeridge to Tyneham Cap, Gad Cliff and Worbarrow. Either up steep hill to Flower's Barrow or into Tyneham, returning via the hill-tops past Grange Arch and Whiteway Farm

Note: Lulworth Range and Tyneham village are open to the public at restricted times. Tel 01929 404819 or visit dorsetforyou.com to check

Just north of the car park and road junction is a sign on the west side of the road to **Lulworth Range Walks**. Follow the path round the south end of a field and then along the ridge to the Range gate. On the way there is a good view of Kimmeridge Bay and Clavell Tower, and as you reach the highest point you may be able to make out the coastguard cottages and chapel at St Aldhelm's Head.

Once inside the Ranges keep strictly to the designated path for your own safety. Proceeding towards **Tyneham Cap** you pass several ruined buildings below on your left, the first being **Shepherd's Cottage** and the next what remains of the settlement of **South Egliston**. Looking north, the more substantial ruins of **North Egliston** can be seen nestling below West Creech Hill; this was traditionally the site of a chapel dedicated to St Margaret.

North Egliston with West Creech Hill beyond.

Note the **drystone walls** of Purbeck Stone, so typical of the area. The unusual **Fiddle Dock**, named after its fiddle-like shape which differs from other species in the genus, can be found by the track during summer. In midsummer look out for **Lulworth** and **Large Skippers**, **Marbled Whites** and **Meadow Browns**, many attracted to the flowering thistles. When you reach **Tyneham Cap**, which is over 180 m high, pause to admire the view.

Tyneham Cap.

The next part of the walk is along **Gad Cliff**, the name referring to a wedge to cleave stone. In late spring you will see colourful flowers such as **Wild**

Gad Cliff.

Clary, **Wild Cabbage** and **Mouse-ear Hawkweed**, with **Wild Thyme** and **Pyramidal Orchid** in early summer. **Wall** butterflies fly up and down the grassland. When **Ravens** became scarce in the 1970s and 1980s, Gad Cliff was their only nesting place in Dorset, but since then they have spread to many other sites.

Wild Cabbage.

The path forks to Tyneham Farm, but keep along the ridge to get a wonderful view of **Worbarrow Bay** from **Gold Down**. Scarce **Field Garlic** may be seen left of the track in late summer and the coconut smell of Gorse flowers in spring is quite powerful.

View of Worbarrow Bay from Gold Down, with the path up to Flower's Barrow seen to the right.

Field Garlic.

The path descends steeply to **Worbarrow Bay and Tout**, the name 'wor' possibly from Old English 'weord' meaning 'watch'. On a raised area above the beach close to the Tout a **display panel** has information on some of the cottages and coastguard station that used to be here. The Miller family lived at Tyneham for over 240 years and there is a legend that they were descended from two Spanish privateers who came over with the

Worbarrow Tout.

Armada in 1588, were wrecked off Scotland and made their way south. The area has been inhabited since prehistoric times. Two large barrows were once visible on the cliffs at Worbarrow and in one of them a Bronze Age pin was found. Evidence of shale working has been found here, with perhaps Purbeck Marble and salt-working industries nearby. Excavations near the cliffs uncovered a floor of chalk blocks, pottery (mostly 1st and 2nd century), sling stones, spindle whorls and a bronze plaque.

The Iron Age hill fort of **Flower's Barrow** stands on cliffs overlooking the bay, though about one-third of it has fallen into the sea. It is reached by a very steep

View from Flower's Barrow.

ascent from the coast path or by walking back to it along the top of Whiteway Hill. The hill fort consists of two main banks and ditches, with the entrance to the south-east, and its appearance suggests two separate stages of construction, with the original univallate (one ditch and bank circuit) earthwork later becoming bivallate (two circuits of ditches and banks). Occupation platforms, which may be hut sites, occur on the north-facing slope of the interior.

When a pit was excavated in 1939, a few sling stones, pottery sherds and bone refuse were found. The local **Durotriges tribe** were probably responsible for developing the fort and it has a commanding view over the surrounding area. The **cross-ridge dyke** to the east, which runs parallel to the eastern ramparts, is almost certainly part of the fortification. A later Roman road may have been constructed from here to Wareham/Worgret. Celtic fields lie to the north.

In 1678 there was a remarkable sighting of an army marching across the hillside from the direction of Flower's Barrow, said to have been witnessed by over 100 people living on the north side of the hill at Steeple and Creech; nothing was seen by the people of Tyneham on the south side. Thinking that an invasion had taken place, word was sent to Wareham, where 300 militia gathered and the bridge was barricaded, while the government in London was put on alert. Nothing more though was heard of the army and it appears to have been a phantom. As well as a substantial number of eyewitnesses there were reports of the sound of 'a great clash of arms'. The army appeared real to the local people of 1678 and it is possible that it was a contemporary phantom (see *Paranormal Purbeck – A Study of the Unexplained* by the author).

If you would like to explore Tyneham, follow the unmade road into the village. On the way you pass a wood consisting mainly of **Ash**, **Elder**, **Sycamore** and **Elm**, with **Wild Garlic** and **Dog's Mercury** as understorey in spring. This is part of **Tyneham Gwyle** (pronounced 'Goyle'; it is an old Dorset word for a

wooded glen near the mouth of a stream or winter torrent) and the Tyneham one was first listed in a charter dated 1648. Willow beds ('withies') were grown in the Gwyle and lobster pots woven from the stems. Burials and pottery fragments from the Iron Age/Roman period have been found near the head of Tyneham Gwyle and seven burials and also a separate skull discovered near the former village rectory. Tyneham is referred to in *Domesday* as 'Tigeham', which may mean 'goat's enclosure' from the words 'tige' and 'hamm'.

Just before the track bears left are some public conveniences and **Tyneham Farm**, with display panels and buildings including a 'history barn' containing an old wagon and picture of Tyneham House above a recreated stage from Tyneham Theatre. The old granary building is closed to the public as three different species of bats roost here. Nearby is a garden with a southerly aspect containing colourful plants.

Beyond the car park lie the majority of the **ruined buildings** – Tyneham was evacuated in 1943 when the army took over the area for military training. Many of the ruined buildings have display panels giving details of the families who lived there. The **school room** is a time capsule containing desks *The deserted village of Tyneham.* of the children and examples of their written work, appropriately related to local nature study; in the corridor is a row of named coat hooks. In late winter/

early spring there is a wonderful display of Snowdrops and Daffodils around the ruined buildings.

Inside the **church** are displays on the history of the village, including farming, fishing, the rectory and school, and also a time line. The ruins of Tyneham House, a Tudor manor built around an earlier medieval building (the south-west wing and hall were 14th century), are not open to the public. In 1683 Nathaniel

The telephone box is a replacement of one dating to 1929 after the original was accidentally destroyed in the 1980s during film-making.

Bond bought the house and the Bond family dominated the village until the army took over in 1943.

Exit the churchyard through the gate on the north-west side and proceed up **Whiteway Hill**. Looking down towards the bay, the building nearby in the field is what remains of **Baltington Farm**. The medieval strip field south of Baltington overlies an earlier Celtic field. In spring there is an abundance of **Bluebells**, **Pignut**, **buttercups** and **Germander Speedwell**. As you climb higher and the turf becomes shorter, such characteristic plants as **Horseshoe Vetch**, **Bird's-foot Trefoil**, **Common Milkwort**, **Mouse-ear Hawkweed** and **Salad Burnet** are apparent in late spring/early summer, and **Hairy Rockcress** grows left of the track in late May/June.

At the top of the hill turn right (unless detouring to Flower's Barrow, in which case turn left) and head eastwards over **Povington Hill**. Below to the left lies the vast expanse of **Povington Heath**, part of the military firing range. The name Povington probably derives from 'Peof's Farm' and there was a mill there at the time of *Domesday*. At Povington Farm evidence was found of a lathe-turned shale armlet industry from Romano-British times and also a hand-cut shale dish or lamp stand.

Povington Hill.

A number of **Bronze Age barrows** are marked on the map and a total of 23 have been recorded on the heath, including three 'bells' and two 'double bowls', though many have been damaged by military activity. Povington Barrow stood over 2 m high and contained a Bronze Age urn, now in the Dorset County Museum. It is interesting that the majority of the barrows in the Tyneham area are on the heath rather than the hills.

As you continue along the hill, look back at the route you have walked from Tyneham Cap. **Bluebells**, **Cow Parsley** and **Greater Stitchwort** grow close to the track in spring. This can often be a good vantage point to note cloud formations and see how clouds are drawn northwards away from the coast.

Povington Hill merges into **West Creech Hill** and there is an old story of how a local girl who hanged herself at Baltington Farm was buried at the boundary between the parishes of Tyneham and Steeple, as suicide victims were not allowed burial in consecrated ground. The area where she is buried is known as **Maiden's Grave Gate** and at one time a tiny coffin was carved into an old oak tree nearby, which subsequently became known as the **Coffin Tree**. Below the hill, to your left, **Povington clay pit** dominates the immediate landscape.

As you approach a small wooded area (**Alms Grove**), cross the Tyneham road and continue on the footpath parallel to the road. **Bluebells** dominate the vegetation in spring.

Exit the Army Ranges and head in the same direction to View Point car park. Go out of the entrance and along the road a few metres before continuing on the track, following the sign to **Grange Arch**. Also known as Bond's Folly, this stands near the top of the Purbeck Hills and overlooks **Creech Grange**, which lies to the north below. It was built by Dennis Bond in the early 18th century as a focal point for the Grange; the Bond family, closely related to the Bonds of Tyneham, owned the latter for about 300 years. Romano-British pottery, quern-stones used for grinding grain and shale waste cores have been found at Creech Grange.

Creech Grange Arch.

From the Arch continue along the hilltop past **Great Wood**. After a while you will see **Creech Barrow Hill** on the left and the barrow on Stonehill Down (Walk 8). At a wooden gate with a notice board about grazing take the sunken path right, downhill, with **Whiteway Farm** below. Some of the buildings date to the late 16th/early 17th century and there was a settlement here in the Iron Age.

At the bottom of the hill turn sharp left and after a short distance bear right through a gate. Follow the path along the edge of a field before coming out on a road. Turn left down the road for a few metres, then take the footpath on the

Creech Grange and heath beyond. The estate includes a farm, chapel and about 120 ha.

right through scrub and trees, which bypasses Whiteway Farm. This brings you out by a stile just west of the farm. The track then heads diagonally south-west across three fields.

In the lower corner of the third field is a wooden **bridge** over **Corfe River**. The track leads into another field, near which is the curious Harp Stone (on *strictly private* land but may be viewable from the public footpath through binoculars). This upright slab of limestone, about 2 m high, with vertical grooves running down it, is known to have been present in medieval times but may have been placed here much earlier. The interesting question is whether the grooves are man-made or simply evidence of natural erosion. It is possible the stone was a boundary marker between the old manors of Hyde and Hurpston and that the latter may have taken its name from the stone.

First references to **Hurpston** are in *Domesday Book* and *Liber Exoniensis* (*Exon Domesday*) as 'Herpere' and 'Harpera' respectively, suggesting 'the harper' (perhaps after the melodious sound of the nearby river). The manor of Hurpston was 275 m east of the stone and there was a mill there in 1086. Later in 1340, 'Herperston' is mentioned in *Nonarum inquisitiones* (documents relating to a unique tax on corn, wool and lamb payable on lay property). There is a local tradition that when the wind blows from the right direction, the grooves on the stone cause a noise similar to a harp.

The track climbs up the field and a small area of downland before reaching a stile. Walk left down the road back to the car park.

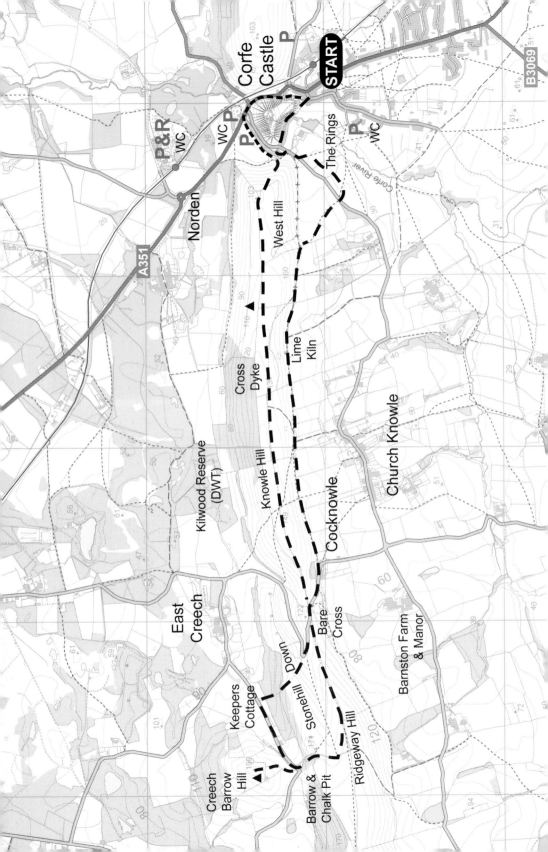

Walk 8:
Corfe Castle to Creech Barrow Hill and Stonehill Down, then Knowle Hill and West Hill

Castles, clay, marl and lime industry relics, sweeping downs, hill-top views and barrows

Distance: approx. 7 miles

Best time to do: any time of year for archaeological features; spring for Stonehill Down wood

Refreshments: various locations in Corfe Castle

Parking: Challow Hill Walkers' car park, Sandy Hill Lane, Corfe Castle (SY 964822), or National Trust Visitor Centre (SY 959825)

Suggested route: Corfe Castle to 'The Rings', skirting West Hill to Cocknowle, then Ridgeway Hill and Creech Barrow Hill, returning via Stonehill Down, Knowle Hill and West Hill

From the village square walk towards Corfe Castle Tea Rooms near the castle entrance and take **Ollie Vyes Lane** to the left round the south side of the castle. There is a good view of the crumbling walls built of Purbeck Stone; the castle was deliberately blown up in the Civil War on the orders of Parliament following a siege when it was defended by Lady Bankes. Excavations in the West Bailey showed traces of an early building, which may have been the royal house at the time of King Edward the Martyr's murder in 978; pottery sherds from the 2nd century have also been found here.

Ravens and **birds of prey** frequently fly over the castle and in summer you may see the small **Lulworth Skipper** butterfly on southern slopes close to the path, as its food plant, **Tor-grass**, can be abundant when grazing has not taken place. This butterfly is mainly confined to south Dorset and can occur in large numbers in some years. **Common Rockrose** is frequent here in late spring/early

Crumbling Corfe Castle.

summer, while later **Burnet Saxifrage** and **Marjoram** adorn the slopes, with some **Common Calamint**.

Wicken Stream (part of Corfe River) is on the left. Saxon 'Wicunstreames' means 'stream of the wicks', with 'wics' probably meaning 'dairy farm'. At the end of the path, cross the road just right of the stone bridge and walk over the wooden bridge. To the right is the former site of **West Mill**, a water mill built in the 18th century, and the earliest one is thought to date to at least 700 years ago.

From the bridge follow the track on the left close to the hedge for about 100 m, then go through a gap in the fence, cross the road and continue on. The earthworks of 'The Rings' (a Scheduled Ancient Monument) are what remains of a Norman **motte and bailey castle**. The smaller ring (the motte) was the strongest part of the castle, with the larger bailey being the area where soldiers were billeted; defence was provided by a ditch, bank and fence system. The Rings are believed to have been built by King Stephen in 1139 when besieging Corfe Castle during the civil war between himself and rival Empress Matilda. In the 17th-century Civil War, Parliamentary forces used the Rings as a base to attack Corfe Castle and it became known as 'Cromwell's Battery'.

Geophysical survey has shown that 'The Rings' were probably built on top of a Saxon field system.

Leave The Rings at a stile in the corner by the hedge, heading west. Cross the road again and follow the sign to Knowle Hill across a field. Exit the field onto a bridleway, turning left along the bottom of **West Hill**. Part of the track is festooned with **Old Man's Beard** and **blackberries** in autumn and **migrant birds** may often be feeding in the bushes. **Stonechats** are resident for much of the year. Look out too for butterflies, including **Marbled Whites**, **Skippers** and **Blues** in open clearings.

The **Gorse** is controlled by burning and grazing by Longhorn and Ruby Red Devon cattle to prevent it swamping other species. The traditional name for the plant is 'furze'. In the Bronze Age it was used in smelting furnaces as it produces high temperatures when burnt but leaves little ash, and later as a fuel in lime kilns, bakers' ovens and brick-firing; also as fodder for horses and cattle; the flowers in flavouring, scent and medicine; bark in dyeing; stems for walking sticks; and seeds as flea repellent. Even the ash has been put to good use in soap-making and fertiliser.

Lime kiln near Church Knowle.

Further along the track is a **restored lime kiln**. Marl, a mixture of clay and calcium carbonate, was burned in kilns to produce lime for mortar and soil improvement.

Continuing along the path, you come to a sign to **Church Knowle**. As its name suggests, the church was built on a mound and in *Domesday* it is referred to variously as 'Cnolle', 'Chenolle' and 'Glole'. Much of the modern village including the New Inn lies south-west of the church. **Cocknowle** is another half mile away and the path here can be quaggy and overgrown; it might be easier to ascend a short way to reach the next stile, before continuing along the bottom.

Pyramidal Orchid.

After a thatched cottage on the left the path rises to an old fenced-off **marl pit**, now containing a number of trees and shrubs such as **Monterey Cypress**, **Ash**, **Common Whitebeam** and **Cotoneaster** species. Follow the path round this, passing through two metal gates, followed by a third near the road, where the tall umbellifer **Alexanders** grows in spring. Do not go through this gate but walk up the narrow track to the right of the fence, where you may see **Restharrow**, **Wild Thyme** and **Pyramidal Orchid** in summer.

At the top you will come to another metal gate at the west end of Knowle Hill. On the right, to the north, an inclined **tramway** (you can still see the gap in the chalk) was constructed in Victorian times to transport marl down to the road, where it was taken to Wareham Cement Works at Ridge to be processed into various limes and also Portland cement.

After passing through the gate, the narrow tarmac road is crossed by several paths. This hilltop crossroads is known as **Bare Cross**. A number of

The view from Ridgeway Hill looking east.

inhumations thought to date from the Roman period were unearthed nearby in 1859 and the graves were found to be parallel and about 30 cm apart; of the six examined, all were thought to be of women or young people.

Walk along the road for a short distance to a wooden gate, which leads onto **Ridgeway Hill**. Below, down the hill to your left and just out of sight, are a number of **pillow mounds** thought to be related to the construction of rabbit warrens in the Middle Ages. **Barnston Farm and Manor** can be seen due south; the house retains much of the original building dating to around 1300 and was probably constructed by a member of the Estoke family, who were associated with the area.

As you climb Ridgeway Hill, **Stonehill Down** is on the right. This saw extensive quarrying by English China Clays in the 20th century and there is a barrow at its western end.

From left to right: Ridgeway Hill, Stonehill Down and Creech Barrow Hill, as seen from Knowle Hill later on in the walk.

At the top of the hill by the metal gate bear right towards the **barrow**. This is oval in shape, with an east–west alignment, nearly 30 m long and 2.7 m high; it is regarded as transitional between long and round barrows on account of its shape and probably dates to the Late Neolithic, being related to long barrows rather than round barrows by its ditch arrangement. There is

Old chalk pit remains on Stonehill Down.

also a disused chalk pit near here.

Creech Barrow Hill is next, reached by returning to the track and taking the left-hand fork after passing through a gate. This brings you onto the road and immediately opposite there is a small lay-by and track leading up the hill. The narrow path takes you through scrub and in spring there is a profusion of **Bluebells**, **Greater Stitchwort** and **Tormentil**. Later in summer the hill is covered with **Bracken**.

'Creech' comes from the word 'cruc' meaning 'hill' or 'barrow', and is one of only a few surviving Dorset words with a Celtic origin. As 'barrow' is Saxon for 'hill', the name 'Creech Barrow Hill' means 'Hill, Hill, Hill'! It is formed of the same material as the lowland heaths – clays, sands and gravels – and has twin peaks, with the southern-most one featuring a **Bronze Age bowl barrow** with a central depression. This barrow is believed to be the one Austen excavated in the 19th century that contained three primary contracted inhumations, one of which had a small, round piece of a child's skull in a flint cairn, showing evidence of trepanning (where a small, circular section of skull was removed to

Creech Barrow Hill.

relieve pressure on the brain, often successfully, by our prehistoric ancestors).

There are also remains of the stone flooring of a building on the hill, thought to be a **hunting lodge** dating to King John's time (1199–1216). Ralph Tresswell's map of 1586 shows a round tower on the summit, and the limestone walls formed a rectangle 9×7.5 m. Pottery sherds from the 16th/17th century and a medieval green-glazed sherd have also been found here. The tower remains are at the centre of a symmetrical arrangement of banks and ditches that form a cross, with the arms running downhill, set within a square over 90 m. From the seat on top of the hill there are fine views.

Retrace your steps carefully (it can be slippery when wet) and when you reach the road, bear left. After partly descending the hill, just after Keepers Cottage follow the sign to **Stonehill Down**. The path ascends south-eastwards through woodland managed by Dorset Wildlife Trust, carpeted with **Lesser Celandine** and **Dog's Mercury** in early spring. The spring flora also includes **Wild Garlic**, **Bluebell**, **Moscatel**, **Goldilocks**, **Early Dog-violet**, **Wood Speedwell**, **Wood Sedge**, **Pignut**, **Wood Anemone** and the uncommon **Toothwort** (near the top of the wood right of the path).

After coming out of the wood go over the top of Stonehill Down, where **Cowslips** grow in spring, and head down towards the eastern end of the valley to a stile accessing the road. Some of these slopes have good grazing and in consequence the sward is shorter, with more flowers such as **Horseshoe Vetch** attracting butterflies like **Adonis Blue** and **Dingy Skipper**.

Climb over the stile and walk up the road in the direction of Cocknowle. Go through the metal gate again to take the Ridge Path back to Corfe

Looking back up Stonehill Down from Cocknowle Gap.

Castle along the top of the downs. As you climb the hill, you pass several undulations which are **Iron Age cross dykes**, which were perhaps settlement or territorial boundaries, the most prominent one being just before the brow of the hill. There was an **Iron Age settlement** between this dyke and one further to the east and finds suggest it was mainly cattle-based, though there was some working of Kimmeridge shale. Within the settlement a roughly circular area about 7.2 m across was dug (perhaps a dwelling) and a floor and coarse pottery have been found. North of the hill lies the Dorset Wildlife Trust reserve of **Kilwood Coppice** and nearby the remains of a **Roman villa** were found, including a tessellated pavement, Tuscan column, pottery and Kimmeridge shale waste.

The walk along the top of **Knowle Hill** provides the opportunity to look down on Church Knowle on the right and gain a perspective of its layout. Just beyond the second metal gate there is another **cross dyke** left of the path with a **Bronze Age bowl barrow** adjoining it; several crouched interments were discovered in this barrow and also antler fragments, pottery sherds and shale, with an extended inhumation near the surface, possibly Romano-British.

The view from Knowle Hill.

About 200 m further on are two more **bowl barrows**, one overgrown and near a stone marker reading 'Corfe 1'. This contained a cist with burnt bones and perforated whetstone above it. The other barrow just north produced a small bronze dagger associated with a primary cremation and two inhumations (probably later) with pottery sherds from the Middle–Late Bronze Age.

Soon after this the main track forks downwards, but continue along the top path, going through a metal gate, followed later by a wooden one, and then head along the top in the direction of the looming castle.

At the summit of **West Hill** are the remains of two more **Bronze Age bowl barrows**, partly fenced off. Nearby, Romano-British pottery sherds (3rd/4th

Bowl barrow on Knowle Hill.

century), 26 Roman bronze coins (mainly from the 4th century but five of earlier date), flint tools and shale lathe waste all indicate some activity at the site. The number of coins suggests a temple or shrine could have been erected,

Corfe Castle from West Hill.

the coins being an offering, and from here the Pagan temples at Norden and Corfe Common may have been visible. There is a bird's-eye view from the barrow, with the edge of **Poole Harbour** near **Swineham** directly north, where there was Roman activity, and **Kingston Hill** directly south, near which a Roman altar was found (Walk 5). Immediately below is a spectacular view of Corfe Castle.

From West Hill descend in a south-easterly direction by some steps. Near the top of the steps you may find **Field Pepperwort** in flower in late spring/ early summer. At the bottom of the hill you can make your way back to the village by the same route you came, or bear left towards the National Trust Visitor Centre and loop back round.

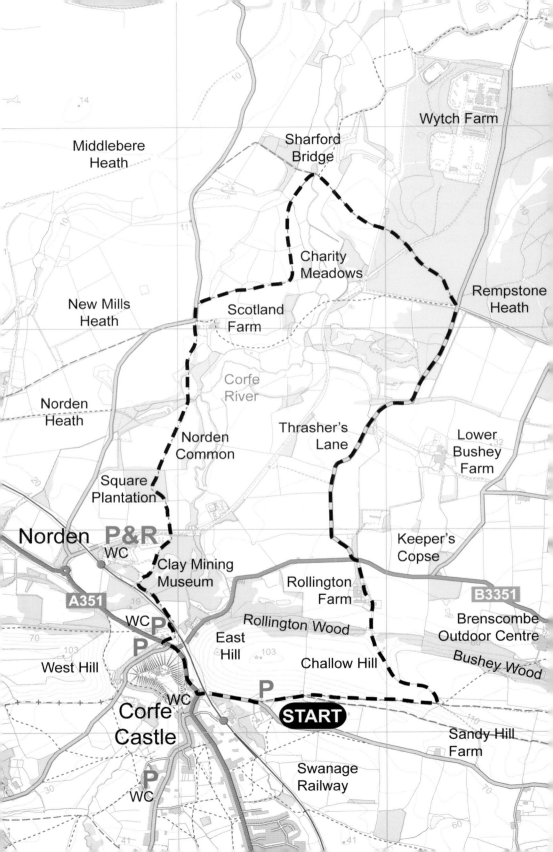

Walk 9:
Corfe Castle to Challow Hill, Sharford Bridge and Corfe Charity Meadows

Scenic views, wild flowers, pine forest, water meadows, old bridge and Purbeck ball clay

Distance: approx. 6 miles

Best time to do: late May–July for Corfe Charity Meadows

Refreshments: in Corfe Castle

Parking: Challow Hill Walkers' car park, Sandy Hill Lane, Corfe Castle (SY 964822), or National Trust Visitor Centre (SY 959825)

Suggested route: up Challow Hill, down to Rollington Farm, Thrashers Lane and Sharford Bridge, through Corfe Charity Meadows to Scotland Farm, Norden Common and back to Corfe Castle

Sandy Hill Lane.

If starting at the NT Visitor Centre, the beginning of the walk is **Sandy Hill Lane** which goes under the railway bridge. **Challow Hill** is accessed through a gate and the Purbeck Way then ascends through mixed scrub and open areas. **Nightingales** are sometimes present in spring and their vibrant song may be heard. Also look out for **Yellowhammers**, **Chiffchaffs**, **Skylarks**, **Buzzards** and **Kestrels**. In late summer/early autumn trees and bushes may hold migrant birds such as **Blackcaps** and **Common Redstarts**.

Wild flowers include **Lesser Centaury**, **Rockrose**, **Elder**, **Dog Rose**, **Horseshoe Vetch**, **Wild Thyme**, **Salad Burnet**, **Pyramidal Orchid**, **Small Scabious** and **Dwarf Thistle**, with rarer **Pale St John's-wort** and **Nit-grass** growing near the track. **Adonis Blue** butterflies

Lesser Centaury.

may be spotted where the turf is shorter and their food plant **Horseshoe Vetch** abounds. **Dingy Skippers**, **Green Hairstreaks** and **Marbled Whites** may be seen near the track.

On reaching the hill-top near the radio mast you will see **Sandy Hill Farm** below to the south with a pond beyond. There is a good view west towards Corfe Castle and the Purbeck Hills, stretching to **Flower's Barrow**. South-west, **Tyneham Cap** stands out in the distance, while **Kingston Church** lies south. The view north-west takes in fields and heath.

The track descending Challow Hill with Corfe Castle in the distance.

Take almost a U-turn and follow the path north-west down the east side of Challow Hill towards **Rollington Farm**. Rollington is referred to in *Domesday* as 'Ragintone', possibly an Old English personal name. The house was built in the second half of the 17th century and the barn and granary date to the early 19th.

The track leads to the main road, to the east of which lies Brenscombe Outdoor Centre; nearby a **Roman villa** was discovered and the remains of two mosaic pavements, also roof and flue tiles, and pieces of brick and pottery from the 3rd/4th centuries. Cross over the main road and take the no-through road known as **Thrashers Lane** (not signed) a few metres to the west, which ends at Wytch Farm where Britain's largest onshore oilfield is situated. There is very little traffic along this road and in late spring/early summer the hedgerows are bright with flowers of **Cow Parsley, Hogweed, Corky-fruited Water-dropwort, Greater Stitchwort, Elder, Honeysuckle, Goatsbeard, Bird's-foot Trefoil, Herb Robert** and **Bush Vetch,** with **Common Fleabane** in late summer.

Thrashers Lane.

After a kilometre or so the soil becomes more acidic and you will see **Scots Pines** and **Foxgloves**. The verge has **Southern Marsh** and **Common Spotted Orchids**, with some hybrids, in late spring/early summer, while in late summer **Common Fleabane, Hemp Agrimony, Water Mint, Dorset Heath** and its hybrid with **Cross-leaved Heath** are present, together with **Dwarf Gorse**. Some **bee hives** and **Grey Squirrels** may be spotted along the way.

Common Spotted Orchid.

Fungus growing along the way.

At a crossroads take the path to Norden, heading north-west through **Scots Pine** woodland. Cross over a road and continue along the track to a gate into a field. As you follow the path north-west across the field you will see **Creech Barrow Hill** in the distance.

The path leads to **Sharford Bridge**, only 1.8 m wide, which dates to about 1700 and replaced an earlier one. The name means 'gap over a ford' and first reference to it is on the Saxton map of 1579 where it is named 'Sherford Bridge'.

Sharford Bridge spanning Corfe River.

Cross over and follow the sign to Scotland Farm, along the river towards the south corner of the field, through **Corfe Charity Meadows**. The water meadow system was constructed in the early 18th century to improve the soil by

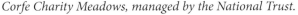

Corfe Charity Meadows, managed by the National Trust.

flooding. These meadows have a rich variety of wild flowers, which is why a visit between late May and July is recommended. The first meadow is especially attractive, with **Corky-fruited Water-dropwort**, **Yellow-rattle**, **Ox-eye Daisy**, **Bird's-foot Trefoil**, **Red Clover**, **Meadow Barley**, **Common Comfrey**, **Chalk Knapweed**, **Lesser Stitchwort**, **Self-heal** and **Rough Hawkbit** putting on a wonderful display; earlier in spring there is an abundance of **Meadow Buttercup** and **Cuckoo Flower**. At the southern end of the meadow is a prominent patch of **Yellow Iris**.

Early Marsh Orchid.

Continue walking in the same direction (south) through a long narrow meadow, which is also full of wild flowers, including **Yellow-rattle**, **Lesser Trefoil** and **Self-heal**. **Marbled White** and **Meadow Brown** butterflies will be flying in summer and dragonflies such as the large **Golden-ringed**. On reaching the third meadow you may see a lovely display of **Early Marsh Orchids** (late May–June), which are a slightly darker colour than the closely related **Southern Marsh Orchid**.

In the third field the path takes a right turn, heading west. At the road turn left and carry on to **Scotland Farm**. The stone in the farmhouse walls was taken from the ruins of Corfe Castle and the name 'scot' refers to a tax or payment..

Go straight on past the farm gate, crossing a boggy area over plank bridges and onto heathland, with **Bog Myrtle** and **heathers**, including **Dorset Heath** and its **hybrid**. After passing through a grove of **Pedunculate Oaks**, **Downy Birches** and **Holly**, the path emerges into an

Cart and wagon restoration by Purbeck Designs and blacksmithing take place at Scotland Farm.

open area with **Bracken**, **Pignut**, **Tormentil** and **rushes**. Follow the path into a small boggy wood, over a stile, then across a large field (**Norden Common**) in the direction of the waymarker arrow towards a gate and stile.

Pass through another wood (Square Plantation). Exit by a stile, followed by a field, keeping left with the castle straight ahead. Another stile leads onto a road. Cross the road and continue on the footpath opposite, round Norden Park and Ride and **Norden Station**, which can be accessed by a gate from the track. **The Purbeck Mineral and Mining Museum** is worth a detour to see

Ball clay museum at Norden.

displays on the clay industry and reconstructed narrow-gauge railway and underground mine.

Purbeck ball clay is a rare deposit consisting of three main minerals found in the area between Corfe and Wareham. There is some evidence that it was used for pottery at Norden in Roman times by the 3rd century. Fine white clay (for pipes) was dug in the 17th century from Povington and Arne Heaths, but it was in the 18th century that it was exploited on a large scale when famous potter Josiah Wedgwood put in large orders after discovering the clay was suitable for his cream-ware. In 1806 the first tramway for transporting clay was opened from Norden to Middlebere run by Benjamin Fayle. The last clay to be dug at Norden was in 1999 when the mine closed. It is used as a constituent for many items and continues to be quarried at several sites in Purbeck and processed at Furzebrook.

As mentioned in the chapter on local history, **Norden** was an important manufacturing centre in Roman times, specialising in high-quality goods such as chalk tesserae for mosaics, carved shale table legs, plaques and Purbeck Marble mortaria. A major Romano-British road connected Norden, perhaps linked to the pottery production site at Worgret, and it is possible the location was chosen for religious as well as practical reasons, since the Durotrigan temple discovered nearby may have already been established in the Late Iron Age, as evidenced by the number of coins found. Earliest reference to Norden is in 1291 ('Northdon'), meaning 'north hill'.

Returning to the route, the path soon bends left parallel with the railway track. Cross the track further along and walk down to the NT Visitor Centre, where there are toilets and refreshments.

Swanage Railway.

Railway trucks waiting at Norden.

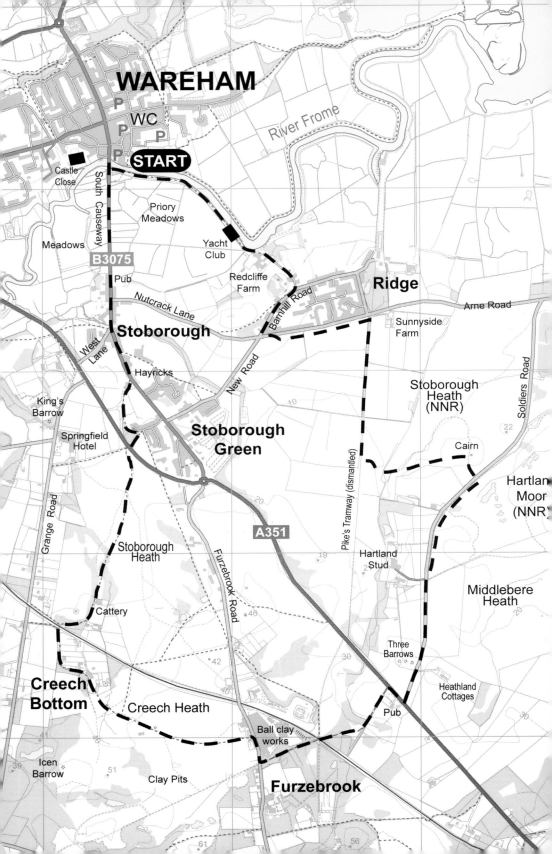

Walk 10:
Wareham to Stoborough, Creech Bottom, Soldiers Road and Ridge

Historic Wareham, wild heathland, the Purbeck Way and River Frome

Distance: approx. 7 miles

Best time to do: summer

Refreshments: many places in Wareham and also the Kings Arms and Halfway Inn on route

Parking: Wareham Quay (SY 924872), except market day (Saturday), or near Sainsbury's

Suggested route: from Wareham across the causeway to Stoborough, on the Purbeck Way to Creech Bottom, across heath to Soldiers Road and Hartland Moor, then Ridge and path by river

Wareham has a fascinating history and it is recommended that the visitor spend some time exploring the town, Saxon walls, churches and museum. The **Quay** has a number of interesting buildings, including the Quay Inn and Old Granary which both date to the 18th century; boat trips can be taken along the River Frome. The present bridge, **South Bridge**, was erected in 1927 and replaced one built in 1777, though there was a much earlier Norman bridge here. When the foundations of the north pier were being dug in 1927, a Saxon sword (now on display in the museum) was found in the river bed.

South Bridge, Wareham.

Before walking south over the causeway towards Stoborough, you pass **Priory Meadow** on the left, which has some display panels on the wildlife that may be seen. The meadows either side of the causeway often flood in winter and are attractive to birds, especially **swans**, **ducks** and **Lapwings**. There is a profusion of **Meadow Buttercup** in spring, while **Meadowsweet** and **Marsh Ragwort** flower in early summer, with **Common Fleabane**, **Purple Loosestrife** and **Reed** blooming later. The large modern building on the mound north-west of the meadows is Castle Close, on the site of the **former 12th-century castle** which featured in the civil war during King Stephen's reign.

Wareham meadows and Castle Close on the site of a Norman castle.

On reaching Stoborough you pass the 17th-century Kings Arms with its thatched roof. **Stoborough** is referred to in *Domesday* as 'Stanberge', meaning 'stony hill' or 'barrow' from 'stan beorg', and there was a mill here at the time. During the Civil War 100 houses were demolished to aid the Parliamentary forces who had taken control of Wareham with a large garrison, but the compensation promised was never paid.

Continue along the pavement, passing Nutcrack Lane; evidence of industrial activity in the Roman period in the form of a clay-lined vat and black burnished ware has been found on the north side of the lane. Go on through the village past West Lane. After several hundred metres take the rough track on the right almost opposite a playing field called The Hayricks. Pass a thatched cottage and bear a little left along the grassy track.

Turn left into a cul-de-sac and round to the right to a Purbeck Way sign to Creech Bottom. Walk along to the busy A351. **King's Barrow** lies west of here, now within the grounds of a private house. It was said to be 3.6 m high and was opened in 1767 when the turnpike road was built. The barrow was composed of layers of turf, and a large hollow oak trunk aligned NW–SE was lying in the centre at the bottom. Human bones (there was no skull) wrapped in deer skins were found in the oak 'coffin', together with a small black urn and some material that may have been gold. This log burial is the only one known from Purbeck and may date to the Early Bronze Age. In 1835 a small barrow nearby was opened and 25 bronze axe heads were found.

Cross the road onto **Stoborough Heath** and bear left on the path. This part of the heath is mainly wet, as shown by **Cross-leaved Heath** (pink flowers June onwards), which attracts the localised **Silver-studded Blue** butterfly, and also clumps of **Purple Moor-grass**. Pink **Lousewort** and blue **Heath Milkwort** can be seen in spring. In drier patches the most obvious plants in early summer are yellow **Tormentil** and tufts of **Bristle Bent** grass, the latter being the food plant of the **Grayling** butterfly, which is on the wing later in summer and likes to settle on sunbaked paths. In late summer **Bell Heather**, **Ling** and **Dwarf Gorse** flower in drier areas. Look out for birds, especially **Stonechat** and **Dartford Warbler**.

Stoborough Heath.

At a junction of paths keep following the Purbeck Way. In wetter areas you may see the pale flowers of **Heath Spotted Orchid** in June. Eventually the path leads to a gate – go through this, past Witch End Cattery, and follow a rough road to the right. You walk past an attractive verge with **Bird's-foot Trefoil** and **Mouse-ear Hawkweed** in early summer and **Common Fleabane**, **Water Mint** and **Hemp Agrimony** later in the season, before reaching the railway track. Cross this and follow the Purbeck Way through the little settlement of **Creech Bottom**.

The path through Creech Bottom.

After passing an area of **Scots Pine** on the right you reach **Creech Heath**. A display board describes how the landscape became open, the wildlife and mining of ball clay. As you follow the Purbeck Way, very wet areas are denoted by the seed heads of

Boggy pool with Oblong-leaved Sundew.

Common Cotton-grass, **Bog Asphodel**, **sundews**, **sedges** and **rushes**. Look for **dragonflies** around the boggy pools.

As the path ascends slightly, a bracken/gorse-clad hillock to the right of the track is what remains of **Icen Barrow**; the name may come from 'isern' meaning 'iron', though it is not clear why it is called that. It is recorded that a Middle Bronze Age urn was found in the barrow. Another barrow was opened on the heath in 1865 and a primary cremation with a garnet-like object found. Immediately south of Icen Barrow is a **clay pit** dug out for the ball clay industry.

Clay pit on Creech Heath, with Creech Barrow Hill forming an imposing backdrop.

Continue along the track before exiting the heath through a small copse. Pass a few houses, part of Furzebrook, and come out onto Stoborough Road. Turn right, walk down the road about 100 m and bear left at a 'crossroads' onto a bridleway. The start of this track can be very boggy. The narrow path goes through trees, with the ball clay processing works on your left, then under the railway track.

The path passes under the Swanage Railway link near Furzebrook.

Go straight ahead on the bridleway onto another part of **Stoborough Heath**. Continue along the path through a wet area with **Yellow Irises**, **Water Pepper** and **Soft Rush**, before coming out on the busy A351 again. Turn right and walk along the verge to the **Halfway Inn**, dating back to the 18th century.

Cross the road and walk down **Soldiers Road** opposite. This is a minor road with little traffic and the verges contain a lot of wild flowers. You soon pass a track on the right leading to red-roofed Heathland Cottages (a National Trust holiday property, formerly an isolation hospital). Further on, left of the road, a gate leads to **Three Barrows**, a group of Bronze Age burial mounds, best viewed before the vegetation has grown up.

Burnet Rose.

Continue along the road, enjoying a variety of flowers from late spring to late summer including **Green-winged Orchid**, **Fragrant Agrimony** (larger and taller than Common Agrimony), **Hogweed**, **Meadow Buttercup**, **Dog Rose**, **Burnet Rose**, **Hemp Agrimony** and **Meadow Vetchling**.

At **Hartland Stud** go through the gate opposite and follow the track on **Hartland Moor** parallel with the road. The moor is a National Nature Reserve known for its birds, reptiles, plants and dragonflies; birds include **Woodlarks**, **Nightjars** and **Dartford Warblers** and reptiles **Smooth Snakes** and **Sand Lizards**. Dragonflies such as **darters**, **skimmers** and **hawkers** may be seen, as well as the more delicate **damselflies**. Rare plants such as **Bog Sedge**, **Allseed** and **Chaffweed** grow here, with more obvious flowers of **Lesser Stitchwort** and **Heath Speedwell** near the track in early summer. Later, **Ling** flowers in profusion, with some **Dwarf Gorse** present, while **Grayling** butterflies patrol the track.

Hartland Moor with Ling and Dwarf Gorse.

In early summer **Southern Marsh Orchid** and scarce **Yellow Bartsia** may be admired along the verge, with **Dorset Heath** and **Devil's-bit Scabious** in late summer. **Stoborough Heath** National Nature Reserve is on the opposite side of the road to Hartland Moor. In boggy areas there are prominent patches of **Oblong-leaved**

Devil's-bit Scabious.

Sundew, **Bog Asphodel** and **Cotton-grass**. **Dragonflies**, especially **Keeled Skimmer** (June–August), favour the boggy pools.

Just after the cattle grid, cross back over the road and head up the grassy hill to the cairn. Bear left around the cairn and follow the elevated path along the edge of the heath.

Cairn on Stoborough Heath above Soldiers Road.

Grazing horses on the heath contribute to better quality vegetation, reduce the risk of fire and increase biodiversity.

After a steep, sandy slide, bear left down to the small stream. Go through a gate and straight towards the electricity pole. **Bog Myrtle**, **Dorset Heath** and **Bog Asphodel** are present near the track. Look for a small sign for Poole

Dorset Heath.

Harbour Trail about 20 m south of the pole, which leads up the bank to the dismantled **tramway**. This narrow-gauge railway was built by the Pike brothers for transporting ball clay from pits they owned at Furzebrook and West Creech to a small quay at Ridge near Wareham on the River Frome. The brothers were in direct competition with Benjamin Fayle who owned Norden clay pits and established the first tramway from Norden to Middlebere (Walk 9). Turn right along the tramway. You may see **Bullfinches** in the scrub and **Marsh and Hen Harriers** quartering the heath in winter.

As the tramway ends, turn left through a gate along the edge of a field parallel with the road. Continue past another gate to the far end. Leave the field and take Barnhill Road to **Redcliffe Farm**. Coarse pottery dating from the 2nd century has been found in a field east of the farm.

Follow the Purbeck Way along the river back to Wareham, past the Yacht Club; many boats are moored here and this may have led to some disturbance to the bird life. **Cetti's Warblers** and **Reed Warblers** still breed and **Kingfishers** may occasionally be seen. The vegetation grows tall by the summer, with **Yellow Iris, Reed, Common Valerian, Common Meadow-rue** and **Common Comfrey** all present, Reed being most dominant in late summer, with **Hedge Bindweed** flowering in profusion in its midst. Day-flying **Scarlet Tiger Moths** may be seen on the wing in midsummer.

River Frome and the Yacht Club near Redcliffe Farm.

You pass a display board on **Percy Westerman**, a prodigious writer of children's books who lived in a houseboat on the Frome, then a panel on how sea levels (the Frome is tidal) and the river landscape have changed over time and, finally, near Wareham, a third information board on some of the wildlife to be enjoyed

The River Frome below Wareham.

References and Further Reading

Natural history and geology

Blamey M, Fitter R, Fitter A (2003) *Wild Flowers of Britain and Ireland*. A & C Black, London.
Bowen H (2000) *The Flora of Dorset*. Pisces Publications, Newbury.
Canning AD, Maxted KR (1983) *Coastal Studies in Purbeck*. Purbeck Press, Swanage.
Chinery M (1991) *Collins Guide to the Insects of Britain and Western Europe*. Collins, London.
Edmonds R (1999) *Fossils*. Dovecote Press, Wimborne.
Green G (2004) *The Birds of Dorset*. Christopher Helm, London.
Hammond C (1985) *The Dragonflies of Great Britain and Ireland*. Harley Books, Colchester.
Harris A, Tucker L, Vinicombe K (1989) *Bird Identification*. Macmillan, London.
Johnson O, More D (2006) *Tree Guide*. Collins, London.
Jonsson L (1992) *Birds of Europe*. A &C Black, London.
Lawrence E, Harniess S (1991) *Letts Pocket Guide to Seashells*. Charles Letts, London.
Pratt EA (2008) *The Wild Flowers of the Isle of Purbeck, Brownsea and Sandbanks*. Brambleby Books, Luton.
Reader's Digest Nature Lover's Library (1982) *Field Guide to the Trees and Shrubs of Britain*. Reader's Digest Association, London.
Reader's Digest Nature Lover's Library (1989) *Field Guide to the Animals of Britain*. Reader's Digest Association, London.
Reader's Digest Nature Lover's Library (1989) *Field Guide to the Water Life of Britain*. Reader's Digest Association, London.
Rose F (2006) *The Wild Flower Key*. Penguin, London.
Thomas J, Lewington R (1991) *The Butterflies of Britain and Ireland*. Dorling Kindersley, London.

History

Calkin JB (1968) *Ancient Purbeck*. Friary Press, Dorchester.
Cox PW (1988) *A Seventh Century Inhumation Cemetery at Shepherd's Farm* (pp 37–45). Vol 110. Proceedings DNHAS. Friary Press, Dorchester.
Cox PW, Hearne CM (1991) *Redeemed from the Heath – The Archaeology of the Wytch Farm Oilfield (1987–90)*. DNHAS Monograph Series 9, Dorchester.
Cunliffe B (1978) *Iron Age Communities in Britain*. Routledge and Kegan Paul, London.
Cunliffe B (1993) *Wessex to AD 1000*. Longman, London.
East Dorset Antiquarian Society (2011) *Article concerning finds in the Football Field at Worth Matravers*. Newsletter Oct 2011.

Field NH (1965) *Romano-British Settlement at Studland, Dorset* (pp 142–207). Vol 87. Proceedings DNHAS. Friary Press, Dorchester.

Gale J (2003) *Prehistoric Dorset*. Tempus Publishing, Stroud.

Green M (2000) *A Landscape Revealed – 10,000 years on a Chalkland Farm*. Tempus Publishing, Stroud.

Grinsell LV (1959) *Dorset Barrows*. Friary Press, Dorchester.

Groves C (1852–1860) Purbeck Society Papers. Purbeck Society, Wareham.

Hardy WM (1910) *Old Swanage, or Purbeck Past and Present*. Dorset County Chronicle Printing Works, Dorchester.

Hearne CM, Smith RJC (1991) *A Late Iron Age Settlement and Black Burnished Ware (BB1) Production Site at Worgret, near Wareham, Dorset (1986–7)* (pp 55–105). Vol 113. Proceedings DNHAS. Friary Press, Dorchester.

Hinde T (ed) (1986) *The Domesday Book – England's Heritage, Then and Now*. Hutchinson, London.

Hinton DA (ed) (2002) *Purbeck Papers*. University of Southampton Department of Archaeology. Oxbow Books, Oxford.

Hutchins J (1973) *History and Antiquities of the County of Dorset, Volume 1*. E.P. Publishing, Wakefield.

Hyland P (1999) *Purbeck: The Ingrained Island*. Dovecote Press, Wimborne.

Keen L (1976) *Bucknowle Farm* (pp 54–62). Vol 98. Proceedings DNHAS. Friary Press, Dorchester.

Ladle L (1994) *Wareham: A Pictorial History*. Phillimore, Chichester.

Legg R (2000) *Corfe Castle Encyclopaedia*. Dorset Publishing Company, Wincanton.

Lewer D, Bernard Calkin J (1975) *Curiosities of Swanage or Old London by the Sea*. Friary Press, Dorchester.

Lewer D, Smale D (1994) *Swanage Past*. Phillimore, Chichester.

Mills AD (1977) *The Place Names of Dorset (Part 1)*. English Place-Name Society University Press, Cambridge.

Papworth M (2011) *The Search for the Durotriges*. The History Press, Stroud.

Parker Pearson M (2005) *Bronze Age Britain*. Chrysalis Books, London.

Putnam B (1989) *Roman Dorset*. Dovecote Press, Wimborne.

Royal Commission on Historical Monuments (1970) *An Inventory of the Historical Monuments in the County of Dorset. Volume 2, South-East Parts 1, 2 and 3*. HMSO, Norwich

Saville RJ (2010) *A Short History of Worth Matravers*. Langton Matravers Local History and Preservation Society.

Stanier P (2004) *Dorset's Archaeology – Archaeology in the Landscape, 4000 BC–AD 1700*. Dorset Books, Tiverton.

Woodward PJ (1980) *A Comparison of Coin Groups from Romano-British Settlements in Purbeck* (pp 102–104). Vol 102. Proceedings DNHAS. Friary Press, Dorchester.

About the Author

David Leadbetter has lived in Purbeck most of his life and spent many years exploring the area on foot, researching and recording different aspects of natural history. Since the late 1980s he has been leading guided walks, through different organisations, including a series of his own local walks. He has been a regular guide on Brownsea Island Nature Reserve and also a volunteer for the Christchurch Countryside Service. He currently volunteers at the Langton Matravers and Purbeck Stone Museum.

With his experience as a teacher and passion for mysteries and local history (in particular the prehistoric period), this is his second book, after *Paranormal Purbeck – A Study of the Unexplained*, published in 2013 by Roving Press and based on interviews with over 100 local people.

Other Books by Roving Press

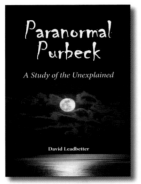

Paranormal Purbeck: A Study of the Unexplained
by David Leadbetter
Footsteps echoing from the past, objects moving of their own volition, near death experiences, displacements in time, memories from the future, UFO sightings, synchronicities ... this book is a collection of remarkable experiences from Purbeck. It visits nearly 70 sites and has contributions from over 100 local people. David challenges fixed opinions and beliefs, offering personal experiences from a small geographical area and arguing that we need a fundamental reappraisal of how we view the world. Anyone with a thirst for mysteries and desire to extend the frontiers of human knowledge will be gripped.

Lesser Known Swanage *by Julie Musk*
Want a different perspective on Swanage? Rather like having your own personal guide, this book offers a close-up view of Swanage – past and present. Packed with surprising facts and stories, with walks suitable for all ages, it will inspire you to explore the town and show you what many visitors and even residents tend to miss. Quotes from local people give a unique insight. An essential read and practical guide for anyone who wants to fully appreciate this friendly seaside town with its wealth of hidden gems.

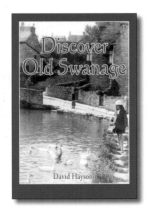

Discover Old Swanage *by David Haysom*
A unique and personal look at Swanage using images from the late 1800s through to the 1980s. David Haysom is Honorary Curator of the Swanage Museum and regularly shares his knowledge of the town on guided walks. Who better to reveal old Swanage? Drawing from his own collection, other personal collections and Museum archives, David's meticulously researched commentary brings each image to life. The book is laid out in seven easy-to-follow walks, with maps to guide you. A delightful trip down memory lane and an absolute must to gain an insight into how Swanage has changed and developed.

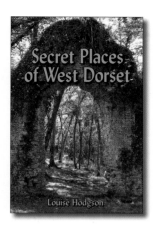

Secret Places of West Dorset
Louise Hodgson

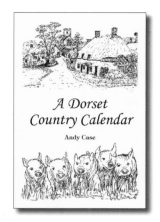

A Dorset Country Calendar
Andy Case

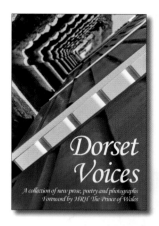

Dorset Voices
A collection of new prose, poetry and photographs
Foreword by HRH The Prince of Wales

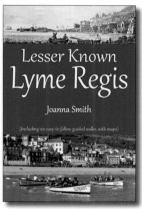

Lesser Known Lyme Regis
Joanna Smith
(including six easy-to-follow guided walks, with maps)

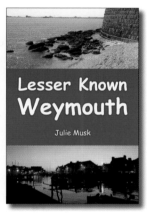

Lesser Known Weymouth
Julie Musk

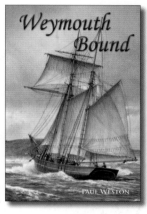

Weymouth Bound
PAUL WESTON

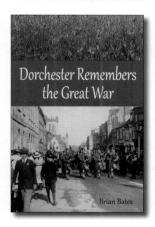

Dorchester Remembers the Great War
Brian Bates

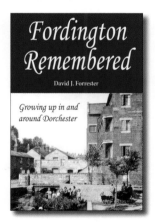

Fordington Remembered
David J. Forrester
Growing up in and around Dorchester

The SPIRIT OF PORTLAND
Revelations of a Sacred Isle
Gary Biltcliffe

Roving Press

www.rovingpress.co.uk
If you like exploring, you'll love our books

*Weathered post on Priest's Way near Acton,
looking back towards Swanage.*